NATIVES WITHOUT A HOME

CANADIAN SOCIAL PROBLEMS SERIES

LONGMAN CANADA LIMITED

Natives without a Home

Mark Nagler

Copyright © 1975 by Longman Canada Limited
55 Barber Greene Road, Don Mills, Ontario

GENERAL EDITOR
Anne-Marie Henshel
YORK UNIVERSITY

Printed in Canada by Web Offset Publications Limited

ISBN 0-7747-3028-5

1 2 3 4 5 6 7 81 80 79 78 77 76 75

In memory of Harry Michaels

Acknowledgements

First and foremost I would like to thank the Native Peoples who have provided me with the encouragement, insight, and interpretations that have made this work possible. I sincerely hope that I have not misrepresented any of the material which they have kindly given me.

I would also like to acknowledge the patient and conscientious editorship provided by Heather Sherratt and Anne-Marie Henshel.

My wife bore the brunt of the frustration associated with the preparation of this work. Her support and direction have been invaluable.

Contents

Foreword

In recent years, the plight of the Native Peoples in Canada—who they are, and what they want—has been drawn to the attention of Canadians. Although the Indians themselves have become increasingly outspoken about their condition and have received wider coverage by the media, many people still have little real knowledge about either the Indians' present conditions or their cultural traditions. Such a book as *Natives Without a Home*, which draws on the author's research experiences with Native Peoples across Canada as well as his knowledge of sociological and other literature on the topic, provides the reader with a well-rounded overview of the Native Peoples' situation in this country.

The literature on inter-ethnic group contact suggests that the categories into which sociologists have classified human beings are not necessarily organized according to objective differences, but rather on developing patterns of differential treatment.[1] For example, although colonists recognized the different languages and customs among the natives, they treated them all as an inferior homogeneous group. That the natives perceived numerous differences among themselves and organized themselves accordingly was of little or no importance to the colonists and made no difference to the way in which they treated natives.

1. T. Shibutani and K.M. Kwan, *Ethnic Stratification: A Comparative Approach*, London: Macmillan, 1972.

At the outset of his analysis, Professor Nagler points out that the Native Peoples do not comprise a traditional ethnic group as do, for instance, the Greeks, Italians or Jews. The distinguishing characteristics of the various groups of Native Peoples, such as language and religion, have hindered their efforts at presenting a united front. Professor Nagler, however, recognizes that how a person is treated depends less upon what he is than on how he comes to be defined. The Native Peoples are collectively labelled as different from white society; they are stereotyped as Tontos, heathens, savages, drunkards—shiftless and lazy—and are effectively treated as such because outsiders find it easier to deal with them in these terms. Athough these stereotypes tend to be inaccurate, they are spontaneously reinforced in a variety of social contexts, with the result that the Native Peoples fulfill these expectations and become the kind of individuals they are believed to be. Thus, while the various Native Peoples are separated by language, customs, and religion, these differences are hardly recognized by outsiders.

Part of Professor Nagler's analysis focuses on the consequences that labelling has for the Native Peoples. The rise of the Red Power movement in Canada, as Professor Nagler suggests, may be viewed as a reaction of the Native Peoples to their perceived intolerable conditions. In his treatise, *The Anti-Semite and the Jew*, Sartre maintained that: "If Jews have a common bond, if all of them deserve the name Jew, it is because they have in common the situation of a Jew, that is, they live in a community which takes them for Jews."[2] It may well be that the unifying element of the Canadian Native Peoples will be their common situation as Native Peoples in a society that treats them as a certain kind of collectivity.

People view the world from a variety of perspectives and from these perspectives try to understand how it works. Each person's behaviour is shaped by the way in which he defines and interprets his respective situation. As Becker maintains, in any hierarchical relationship in which the parties concerned attempt either to maintain or to change the existing relations of power and authority, conflicting definitions of the situation will

2. J.P. Sartre, *The Anti-Semite and the Jew*, New York: Schocken Books, 1965, p. 67.

inevitably occur.[3] We can, therefore, reasonably expect that the Native Peoples' interpretation of their condition will differ from that of the various government agencies that deal with them. Becker's notion of a hierarchy of credibility refers to the phenomenon whereby in any system of ranked groups, "participants take it as given that members of the highest group have the right to define the way things really are."[4] It is also assumed that members of the subordinate groups do not have sufficient information about the total situation and therefore their view of reality is partial and distorted.

Professor Nagler's focus in this book provides the reader with a sympathetic understanding of Native Peoples. The value patterns of native life are documented to illustrate how the values of traditional native society enable the Native Peoples to adjust to their environments. For example, the author discusses Native Peoples' mutual aid system, their concept of time, and their attitudes towards public secular education. Because their value systems differ from those of the larger society, they are misunderstood by and unable to adjust to that society. When, for example, Native Peoples object to and strongly resist the kind of public education traditionally offered in the host society's schools, they are considered poorly motivated towards achievement and success. It is only when we realize, as Professor Nagler suggests, that the Native Peoples' cultural interpretations of these activities are different from ours, that we can appreciate and understand their objections and resistance.

Native Peoples, in our society, are coming more and more into contact with outsiders. The insulating mechanisms that were effective in the past are less successful in a society in which the influences of modern technology have spread into all sectors of society. As Becker has stated: "Since there are generally several categories of participants in any social organization or process, we must choose between taking the viewpoint of one or another of these groups or the viewpoint of an outside observer."[5] If we

3. H.S. Becker, *Sociological Work: Method and Substance*, Chicago: Aldine, 1970, p. 126.
4. Ibid., p. 126.
5. Becker, *Outsiders: Studies in the Sociology of Deviance*, New York: The Free Press, 1963, p. 1972.

are to understand the condition of the Native Peoples, we must first attempt to understand their point of view. Professor Nagler's analysis of the Native Peoples from their own perspective must therefore be seen as a welcome move towards such an understanding.

October, 1974   Bill Shaffir
DEPARTMENT OF SOCIOLOGY
MCMASTER UNIVERSITY

Introduction

North American Indians, although the sole indigenous American people, are now natives without a home. As the early European settlers in North America gradually acquired the more productive lands for themselves, the native Indians withdrew or were driven from their traditional homes. As a result, social systems eventually evolved in which the rights, privileges, and duties of the Native Peoples[1] were defined by the new arrivals, who had become the dominant group. This pattern of European settlement, which forced the native inhabitants to withdraw further and further into the hinterlands, can be seen in several countries. To a greater or lesser extent this happened in New Zealand with the Maoris, in Australia with the Aborigines, and in South Africa with the original black tribesmen.

The patterns of relationship between the native groups and the newcomers can vary, however. Although the two groups may co-exist peacefully for some time after the initial settlement, a stratification system eventually develops, with the Native Peoples at the bottom of the hierarchy. In cases where legal sanctions were imposed, the Native Peoples suffered severe deprivation. For example, in Canada the *Indian Act* designated the Native Peoples as different from the rest of the Canadian population, with separate rights and privileges. The native

---

1. The term "Native Peoples" is perhaps the best term to describe North American Indians as this segment of the population does not constitute, in the sociological sense, an ethnic group.

groups in some instances were isolated physically and socially, as well as legally, from the dominant social groups, and in others they were enslaved or even eliminated, as was the case with the Beothuk Indians of Newfoundland. Although in many parts of Canada the Native Peoples remained in close proximity to white settlements, they were effectively isolated by the reserve system. This isolation enabled the Native Peoples to maintain many of their traditional culture patterns (although in modified form). However, it also meant that their culture tended to atrophy from lack of external stimulation, for the reserve system isolated the native groups not only from white settlers, but also from other native groups.

The Indians often encountered considerable prejudice if they left the reserves and tried to join the mainstream of Canadian society. This colour or class barrier resulted from the ethnocentricism of the white settlers, who tended to see the values of their group as the absolute standard for judging all other groups in society. Those behavioural patterns that differed from the settlers' standards of proper conduct were considered inferior.

The focus of this study will be on the major factors that have been influential in the Native Peoples' adaption to Canadian society, in their awareness of their inferior position, and in their attempts to make the social distances between themselves and the dominant society more flexible. Because the legal definition of Indian does not include a large proportion of those who are of Indian descent and who may live under the same conditions as treaty Indians, in this study the term "Indian" or "Native Peoples" will extend to all people of Indian ancestry.

Partly because of their comparatively small numbers and partly because of their traditionally "inferior" position, the Native Peoples form a relatively invisible minority in Canadian society. Although Canadians usually view themselves as racially liberal and often are critical of racial policies in countries like South Africa, the Soviet Union, and the United States, they cannot in fact take much pride in their past treatment of their own minorities. There is considerable evidence that Canadians have treated the Native Peoples and the Japanese of Canadian descent as negatively as many of the countries they criticize have treated minority groups.

The majority of Canadians seldom come into contact with the Native Peoples. For them, "Indians" exist as myth (images of Tonto, warriors, savages, heathens), since the Native Peoples have not until recently been in a position to make an impact on North American society. Because of the Indians' social and physical isolation the majority of Canadians are not aware of the conditions under which most of the native population lives. Before the relationship between the two groups can change, there must be more understanding and awareness of these conditions. An extended transitional period of trial, error, and experimentation is needed to achieve any consensus between the groups. Such a transitional period is already occuring in some of the newly independent Black African countries, in the Black Power groups in the United States, in the Middle East, Ireland, the Caribbean and South American states. These movements have tended to give minority groups the impetus to gain rights and privileges enjoyed by those in power.

Before we can examine how the Native Peoples are affected by the prejudices and ethnocentricism of the dominant society and how they are trying to gain their rights, it is necessary first of all to define what is meant by the term "Native Peoples", and secondly to establish how these people are classified and evaluated in Canadian society. There is still considerable controversy among sociologists about whether the Canadian Indians constitute an ethnic group or a cultural minority. Unlike most other minorities in Canada, the Native Peoples do not share a common cultural tradition; their lifestyles vary widely according to their geographical and traditional backgrounds. If one examines, for example, French Canadians, Italians, Japanese, or Chinese, one finds that people in each group share common features (such as language and tradition) which help to create their sense of identity as a distinct group. The Canadian Native Peoples, on the other hand, have many different cultural traditions. In some cases, Indians of the same tribe speak different dialects because they are separated geographically. Because they do not have any strong sense of group identity, the Native Peoples find it difficult to formulate common policies and to organize themselves at the local, provincial, or federal levels. Their diversity has tended to preclude the development of organizations and leaders who can legitimately represent the whole group. Lacking this sense of community, small groups of the Native Peoples have developed individual conceptions of which policies would best serve their interests.

It is difficult to analyse the Native Peoples from a sociological point of view as precisely as the traditionally defined ethnic or minority groups, since they differ from most other groups not only in that they lack a sense of identity, but also because they have not been assimilated into the larger society to the extent that many groups have. If one examines other minority groups in Canada, such as the Ukrainians, Hungarians, or Germans, one finds that these groups have adopted the basic values of Canadian society. As a result, they are more likely to be able to participate in the society at all levels, although they still may encounter prejudice in some areas. The Native Peoples, on the other hand, have not associated with this society; they have been isolated physically and culturally so that a large proportion of them have not had the chance to assimilate any patterns of Canadian life. Therefore they are more prone to encounter difficulties, since they are in the society without being part of it.

Although Native Peoples do experience difficulty in crystallizing goals and policies for their collective benefit, the land-claim actions and the formation of Red Power groups show that they are beginning to see themselves as a distinct group. They are starting to concentrate their attention on those features they share, especially on the fact that they are all descendants of the original North American inhabitants. Although they possess many different cultural and social traditions, their position in North American society can be seen as the factor that unifies them as a sociological entity.

As has been pointed out, many factors make it difficult for the Indians to assimilate into North American society. The aim of this study is to clarify the position of the Native Peoples as a minority group in Canada today, and to examine how they are reacting to their situation. Chapter 1 examines the significance of identity and the way in which native status and identification are a consequence not only of legal definition but also of self-definition, folklore images, and stereotypes.

The Native Peoples' fear that their traditional cultural patterns are being destroyed, and their attempts to perpetuate their ancestral ways of life, are explored in Chapter 2. Some of these people have assimilated or are attempting to assimilate Western traditions, and others are attempting to unite their diverse cultural patterns in the emerging movement known as Pan-Indianism. However, many still encounter difficulties if they move to urban communities because their cultural patterns are at variance with those of the larger society.

The problems that the Indians have encountered in the Canadian educational system are examined in Chapter 3. In many cases, Indians have received little sympathy from the relatively unqualified teachers who have to work with curriculae which bear little relevance to the native experience. Some authorities have maintained that, because of their cultural poverty, the Native Peoples are as handicapped as other poverty groups in attaining the benefits of education.

Chapters 4 and 5 examine the consequences of the reserve system. Native religious observances, political consciousness, and the development of the Red Power movement have been shaped in part within this context. As shown in Chapter 5, the Native Peoples, although diversified, are gradually developing a positive self-image which is producing better organization and leaders. They are thus enabled to exert a more powerful and unified impact on Canadian society than ever before.

The inducements for many of the Native Peoples to move to urban centres and the consequences of these moves are discussed in Chapter 6. Chapter 7 explores particular difficulties that Native Peoples encounter in urban society and the deviant behaviour to which many of them resort. Findings show that the deviant patterns examined are not uniquely Indian, but apply to most lower socio-economic groups in society. The concluding chapter attempts to define the position of the Native Peoples in Canadian society at the present time, and to examine whether their growing self-awareness as a disadvantaged group has in any way altered their condition.

1 Identification and Social Status

One of the major difficulties facing the North American Indians today is their lack of a sense of group identity. It is this consciousness of kind or "ethnicity" that is the main cohesive factor of most ethnic or minority groups; and it results from an awareness that members of a group share a common cultural pattern in which the traditions, folklore, values, and religion or beliefs usually derive from a common ancestral background. Many of the immigrant groups, such as the Poles, Greeks, Ukrainians, or Italians, feel themselves bound together because they have more in common with other members of their own group than they have with the larger society. Although there may be wide differences of background and beliefs within an ethnic group, these are of lesser importance than the similarities.

This is not the case with the Native Peoples. Before the white settlers arrived in North America, the Native Peoples did not think of themselves first as Indians and then as members of a particular tribe; they thought of themselves as Cree, Blackfoot, Algonquin, etc. Native Peoples do not have a common physical, social, or cultural background, but rather have a wide range of traditional cultures that have been designated as "Indian culture" by white people viewing it from the outside.[1]

What are considered to be the distinguishable characteristics of native cultures are in essence abstractions of significant cul-

1. M. Nagler, Indians in the City, Ottawa: Canadian Research Centre for Anthropology, 1970, p. 19.

tural and social forms which have been observed among segments of the Indian population. These various tribal traditions produced a number of unique Indian cultures which once overlayed the populated areas of North America like a finely patterned mosaic but which appeared to non-Indians to be nothing more than a patchwork of unrelated pieces. Since the arrival of the white man, the Indian cultures have been subject to what some anthropologists call "deculturation," the result of the imposition of alien ideas and values.

We are, therefore, dealing with two radically different points of view: that of the Native Peoples themselves who perceived the differences rather than the similarities between the tribes; and that of the outsiders or white people who preferred to see the Indians as one cultural group. Since the white population has become the dominant group in North American society, their perspective has been adopted as the norm and the Native Peoples have had to try to adjust to these alien standards. Hallowell defines this process of adaptation which he calls "transculturalization" as a process whereby individuals are temporarily or permanently detached from one group and come under the influence of the customary ideas and values of an alien society.[2]

There are two polar segments of this transculturalization process that create a conflict between involvement with one's own cultural grouping and the pressure to become part of the dominant society. The Native Peoples who still retain some of their own cultural identity tend to be located on reserves. Some Native Peoples inevitably come into contact with North American society and try to assimilate—a process which involves a cultural readaptation in which they have to, at least on a superficial basis, discard the culture, values, and social practices of their native society and adopt those of the larger community. Complete transformation is seldom desired by any minority entering a new society or seldom permitted by the majority, which wishes to retain its separate and unique position. According to Hallowell, the degree of transculturalization depends on a number of variables:

2. A. Hollowell, "American Indians, White and Black: The Phenomenon of Transculturalization," *Native Americans Today: Sociological Perspectives*, H. Bahr, B. Chadwick, and R. Day, eds., New York: Harper and Row, 1971.

... the age at which the process begins; the previous attitudes towards the people of the second culture; the length of residence, the motivational factors, and the nature of the roles played . . . . Thus Indianness is a specific example of the wider human phenomenon of transculturalization which occurs in any society where minorities encounter the ruling group.[3]

Transculturalization is not, however, always a one-way process, but depends on the expediences of the moment. This can be seen if we examine the four stages into which E. P. Patterson divides the Indians' relationship with Europeans.[4] The initial stage of contact was one in which the Native Peoples achieved prosperity as they provided the Europeans with needed goods and services. During this period, the natives were able to keep their independence, and the patterns of association were mutually beneficial to both parties. The North American Indians therefore maintained their cultural patterns during this time because their "technology" was superior or better adapted to the environment than that of the newcomers.

Patterson maintains that the initial stage was followed by an era in which European economic interests developed at an unprecedented rate. The Native Peoples continued to greet the white men with hospitality, since they did not realize the aims and intentions of their guests. They still believed that the Europeans were coming as visitors, not as invaders. Patterson maintains that:

... far from having a common sense of identity and purpose, Indians were very diverse in their political groupings, though they were nearly all hunters and gatherers. Differences in language and religion meant that they responded to the Europeans according to their own needs and ambitions.

To the Europeans, however, their resemblances outweighed their differences. This may be, in part, a reflection of the Europeans' notion of the Indians' role in the European economy which was primarily their ability to provide furs.[5]

---

3. *Ibid.*, p. 205.
4. E.P. Patterson, *The Canadian Indian: The History Since 1500*, Toronto: Collier-Macmillan, 1972.
5. *Ibid.*, p. 59

This soon developed into the third stage—an era of dependency in which the Indians became bound in a trade relationship that eventually made them economic slaves of the Europeans. As Native Peoples devoted more time to providing for the needs of the Europeans, they tended to spend less and less effort continuing their own traditional patterns of life. This economic reliance weakened their traditional ties, and they became dependent on the Europeans for military assistance. At the same time, increased European immigration resulted in the Native Peoples being displaced from large tracts of land. They were subsequently put on reserves which eventually became aboriginal communities. This process resulted in the Native Peoples becoming dependent on the white man for their economic, political, and even their social existence. The regulations to which those on reserves were subject tended to be enforced in a harsh manner by the official agents of the government, who seldom empathized with native life patterns. Many of these agents not only enforced the provisions of the Indian Act, but also insisted that their personal directions be obeyed without question. They were often in a position to apply sanctions if their directives were not followed.

In Canada, the fourth period began in 1876, the year that the first *Indian Act* was passed. By this time, the Indians were no longer valuable to the newcomers in terms of providing important goods or services to the society. Patterson continues:

> ... *the European made himself into the native and the Indian was transformed into an ethnic group. It is interesting to speculate on the consequences of the development of this ethnicity.... As a minority in his own land, the Indian saw the European as a coercive and superimposed majority who were not inheritors of the space they occupied, but the usurpers of Indian land and the destroyers of Indian rights and heritage.*[6]

This stage was marked by the Indian population's decline, their substantially lower standards of living, and their depen-

6. *Ibid.*, p. 40.

dency on the welfare system. During this period as well, the Native Peoples lost their political independence and social integrity. They found themselves playing the role of outcasts in a land where they had once been sovereign. The third phase had the effect of destroying or at least severely damaging many native cultural institutions.

Many anthropologists and sociologists maintain that the majority of Native Peoples did not adopt Western customs. As Patterson maintains:

. . . because individuals assimilated in Canadian society and because the Indian culture clearly was not what it had been at its earliest European contact, non-Indians assumed that Indians were being assimilated. This understanding of the situation served to underscore the prevalent view of Indian culture as static and encouraged the tendency to interpret all changes as evolution towards assimilation, rather than a creation of a new synthesis which continued to be "Indian culture."[7]

The destruction of Indian group identity became an established pattern that did not begin to reverse until the emergence of the new philosophy which stressed equality and pride in racial identity and culture.

Patterson implies that the third stage closed at the end of the second World War, but it appears that the third phase did not end until the late 1950's, prompted by the evolution of the civil rights drive in the United States and the independence movements in several colonial countries. During this period, the Native Peoples began to acquire a new and positive identity. In its most radical form, this identity expressed itself in the Red Power movement, which was intended to emulate the Black Power movement's efforts to achieve rights which had been lost by the Black minority group. The most radical manifestation of the Red Power movement was the Wounded Knee incident in 1973, where a group of Native Peoples barricaded themselves in a small town in South Dakota for over two months, costing the

7. *Ibid.*

government of the United States more than two million dollars. The Native Peoples hoped that this incident would begin to make government authorities as well as the population at large aware of the Indians' difficulties.

With the advent of the fourth phase, a sense of positive Indian identity is beginning to emerge. The Red Power movement is, in part, a reaction to the second-class citizen image of the Indian projected by books, magazines, movies, radio, and television. Inevitably, a large number of the native population have identified with this image, and pressures of negative evaluation have inhibited the Native Peoples' drive towards self-determination. However, Native Peoples are now collectively endeavouring to change the Hollywood image of the "North American savage." Positive identity has been slow to emerge because of many internal disagreements, but this in fact may prove to be a blessing. Perhaps in working out their difficulties and working toward uniformity of commitment, their place in American society will be more firmly established. As a cohesive group, they may achieve goals that diverse groups of the Native Peoples have been seeking for some time.

Present legislation on Indian affairs does not, however, greatly improve the status of Indians, although cases are now being fought in the courts which could open the way to better legislation. The *Indian Act* of 1952 defines a Canadian Indian as "a person who persuant of this Act is registered as an Indian, or is entitled to be registered as an Indian."[8] This definition is very narrow, since it does not include enfranchised Indians who, because they or their ancestors renounced Indian status, are no longer entitled to the special rights and privileges accruing to those with the legal status of Indians. Rights extended to non-enfranchised Indians include the right to live on the reserve and to receive monies. Treaty Indians—or "legal Indians" — supposedly have the right to free medical care, free education, freedom from income tax for all funds earned on the reserve, and freedom from property tax on the reserve. For many, the reserve is also a home to which they may return at any time and in

8. *The Indian Act*, R.S.C., 1952, C149, as amended by 1952-53, C41 and 1956, Department of Citizenship and Immigration, Ottawa 2, (1, g).

which, theoretically, their minimum necessities will be guaranteed under the provisions of the *Indian Act.*

Indians may choose enfranchisement for a number of reasons. The most important of these appears to be economic, for when Native Peoples voluntarily renounce their Indian status they are given a certain sum of money. Women, however, automatically lose their Indian status when they marry men who are not registered as Indians, and their children are not considered Indians under the terms of the *Indian Act.* This provision is currently being tested in the courts. On the other hand, when men of legal Indian status marry non-Indians, their spouses acquire Indian status, as do their offspring.

In Canada, there are 571 Indian bands living on 226 reserves throughout the country. In some instances, as is the case in British Columbia, a band may be allocated to more than one reserve. The term "band" refers to a number of Indians organized as a group which is so recognized by the Canadian government. The term "reserve" refers to the land inhabited by a band of Indians. Indians resident on reserves are banded; that is, they are registered as being members of the band on the official band list. The official register is kept in Ottawa and only persons whose names appear on this register are entitled to be designated "Indians" in the legal sense.

This legal definition is obviously too narrow, as there are many Canadians of Indian descent who are not deemed Indians in the legal sense. Many non-treaty Indians live in areas outside the cities, usually on the outskirts of small towns, since they are legally prohibited from living on the reserves.

Native Peoples in Canada have, in this way, been legally defined as different from other citizens of Canada and have been to a large extent isolated from the mainstream of society through the reserve system. Theoretically, these communities were intended to permit the natives to live according to their traditional patterns of life, but in practice, most reserve areas provided only minimal resources which made a viable independent existence impossible. And because the Native Peoples were not trained or equipped to adapt to modern society, they eventually became dependent on the welfare system.

Although the reserve system effectively prevented the Native

Peoples from taking any active role in the dominant society, some form of cultural contact was inevitable. This contact did not, however, result in the Native Peoples' assimilation or acculturation in the larger society, but rather helped to widen the gap and emphasize the differences between the two groups. Because of this lack of knowledge and sympathy, the majority of Canadians tend to hold what may be called folk images of the Native Peoples. These images generally take two contrasting forms, but both view the Indian as the remnant of a population that is fast disappearing. The negative image of the Indian is of a Tonto figure, a heathen warrior who hindered the progress of pioneer expansion, a drunk, a misfit, or a welfare case. The positive image depicts the Native Peoples as part of the North American folklore and traditional heritage whose culture and art must be preserved. Both these views depend to a large extent on the kind of contact the non-Indians have had with the Native Peoples. Those living near the Indian reserves or in cities with large communities of non-treaty Indians on the outskirts tend to take the negative point of view, whereas people living in the larger urban centres such as Montreal, Toronto, Edmonton, or Vancouver, where contact with the Native Peoples is almost non-existent, tend to hold the more idealized view. As Jean Elliott says, the state of the Native Peoples' identity at least in part, is a result of the kind of cultural contact they have with the rest of society:

> ... the majority of Canadians may esteem the art of native peoples, but their appreciation of it is from their own vantage point, removed from the total cultural pattern from which it had its origins. The native people on the other hand, are becoming increasingly acculturated in that they are taking on the dress, language, customs, and values of the dominant society. In time, there will be few cultural reminders of the precultural contact era, which are not in the same way reflecting the unequal influence of both cultures. In fact, this is a trend which is potently demonstrated by Canadian Indians. However, this atrophy of their basic cultural practices is not correspondingly relinquished in their self-definition.[9]

9. J.Elliott, Native People, New York: Prentice-Hall, 1972, p. 2

In summary, the Canadian Native Peoples do not enjoy the same advantages enjoyed by most other Canadian ethnic groups, such as the Italians, Ukrainians, or Chinese: they do not have the consciousness of kind that emanates from the same cultural, social, or political background and a general sympathetic identification with others in the same category. As Shibutani and Kwan state, "the history of any group consists of those collective memories shared by its members of the deeds of their ancestors, of their glories and persecutions, achievements and failures."[10] This agrees with Hughes and Hughes' definition of an ethnic group as consisting of those who conceive of themselves as being alike by virtue of their common ancestry, real or fictitious, and who are so regarded by others.[11]

But this definition does not apply to the Native Peoples of Canada in the same way that it can be applied to most other minority or ethnic groups. However, an ethnic identity is being imposed on Native Peoples — partly through their own awareness of how they are viewed by others, but mainly through the pressure of the larger society on them to see themselves as a different and separate group.

10. T. Shibutani and K.M. Kwan, *Ethnic Stratification: A Comparative Approach*, London: Collier-Macmillan, 1963, p. 43.
11. *Ibid.*

2 Patterns of Culture

As discussed in the previous chapter, the Native Peoples have been separated from the rest of the Canadian population—either on reserves or, in the case of the non-treaty Indians, in settlements on the outskirts of larger cities. This physical separation has served to maintain a social, psychological, and cultural isolation which in many respects has inhibited the realization of typical urban or white value patterns in native societies. As will be discussed in subsequent chapters, the Native Peoples have encountered considerable prejudice and discrimination when they have attempted to assimilate in the larger community.

One of the factors that has fostered separation between Native Peoples and other Canadians is the fact that the Native Peoples often distrust the agreements, customs, and manners of white society. They generally believe that treaty agreements are maintained by whites only as long as they serve white interests. This situation is currently illustrated in the case of the James Bay Development, where treaty rights supposedly granted to the Native Peoples appear to have been disregarded in the interests of white economic development. On November 15, 1974, the Quebec government awarded the Cree and Innuit Peoples one hundred fifty million dollars, a twenty-five thousand square mile area in which traditional hunting and fishing rights will be preserved, and the promise that Native Peoples will be involved in the James Bay scheme. This decision probably will set a precedent for the acknowledgement of native rights. While this compensation appears generous, one must be aware that it might further contribute to the destruction of aboriginal life.

Sociologists in the nineteenth century generally assumed that, like other minority groups, the Native Peoples would gradually be absorbed by the mainstream of Canadian society in spite of their physical, cultural, and social separation. It was expected that as white society expanded and took over the Indians' traditional lands, acculturation would accelerate and encompass every aspect of Indian culture. Just as the immigrant groups had been Canadianized, so would the melting pot process absorb the Native Peoples—to the extent that the Indians as such would be a vanishing race. In fact their geographical and social separation from white society meant that the Native Peoples were able to maintain at least some aspects of their original culture and identity. Although their social structures, religions, and languages have undergone some changes because of social contact with Canadian society, they have not been acculturated to nearly the same extent that most immigrant groups have been, and, apart from the Beothuk tribe of Newfoundland, they have by no means disappeared.

Evon Z. Vogt, in his article, "The Acculturation of American Indians," advanced a conceptual framework for the analysis of this process of acculturation.[1] His thesis suggests that, in order to understand the acculturation processes of Native Peoples and other tribal groups, one must take into consideration the nature of the two cultures involved as well as the conditions in which contact occurs. Attitudes towards strangers, the type of sociocultural integration, settlement patterns and the intercultural compatibility of settlement patterns must be considered, along with "such questions as whether the contact is forced or permissive, of long or short duration, intensive or sporadic, and so forth."[2]

The process of acculturation, Vogt maintains, may be either microscopic or macroscopic. It is microscopic if there are recur-

---

1. F. Z. Vogt, "The Acculturation of American Indians," *Annals of the American Academy of Political and Social Science*, May, 1957. Reprinted in *Perspectives of the North American Indians*, M. Nagler, ed., Ottawa: Carleton Press, 1972, pp. 2-13.
2. *Ibid.*, p. 4

ring sequences of events "such as the diffusion of concrete objects between two cultures," for example, if stone tools are replaced by steel axes.[3] The macroscopic process, according to Vogt, includes the more pervasive patterns of change that persist over long spans of time and that involve alterations in the basic socio-cultural systems.

The microscopic process involves simple additions, subtractions, or replacements of one cultural or linguistic content by another; the macroscopic process is more concerned with structural and pattern changes. Vogt terms the microscopic changes additive or fusional, whereas the macroscopic are isolative, nativistic, or assimilative. There are also a number of factors which may inhibit complete acculturation, such as isolation or discrimination, especially in education and employment. These limiting factors account for the persistence of native cultures in spite of the ever-increasing pressures from white society towards full acculturation and the complete assimilation of native populations. White society has never completely accepted minorities and, in many instances, will reject minorities even though they may have basically the same cultural patterns and values as the host society.

> ... the argument has often been advanced ... that isolation of the Indian populations on remote reservations administered by the Indian Bureau has insulated them from proper exposure to educational facilities, mass communications, and so forth and has prevented them from obtaining the means for assimilation. This hypothesis has undoubted merit, but it certainly fails to account for the many cases of Indian groups which have been subjected to a great deal of contact with white society, yet who continue to maintain many of their old patterns.[4]

Dozier advanced another hypothesis to account for this lack of complete acculturation.[5] He maintains that if forced accultura-

---

3. *Ibid.*, p. 5.
4. *Ibid.*, p. 8.
5. E. Dozier, G. Simpson, and N. Yinger, "The Integration of Americans of Indian Descent," *Annals of the American Academy of Political and Social Science*, May, 1957.

tion does not lead to early absorption of the subordinate group, there will be a high degree of resistance to change in the indigenous cultural patterns. As far as Canadian Native Peoples are concerned, this hypothesis appears to be exemplified by the Haida of British Columbia and the Iroquois of Ontario and Quebec. The socio-cultural systems of these native groups were highly organized, so that they were able to develop patterns of resistance when forced acculturation was attempted.

According to Vogt, a further explanation for failure to *assimilate* involves a theory about the nature of culture. This thesis maintains that, while the material aspects of a culture can undergo change without difficulty, family, kinship, and other social institutions are of a more persistent nature and "the aspect of the way of life which has been labelled as a core culture, implicit values, cultural orientations and personality type are still more persistent."[6] This hypothesis does apply to some native groups but it does not account, as Vogt points out, for "the variability we observe in rates of change in different aspects in American Indian culture."[7] Neither does it answer the basic question of how any patterns of Indian culture can be preserved, considering the kind and degree of pressure for change that many Indian tribes have experienced.

The fact remains that no minority group has become completely integrated into Canadian society and that there are always barriers to full acculturation. Many groups maintain their social and cultural traditions through organizations designed to preserve their heritage. For example, the Chinese, Italians, and other minority groups form various folk societies. For Native Peoples, this is more difficult to do because they do not have the same feeling of ethnic identity as other minority groups have. Nevertheless they have started to organize themselves in the Pan-Indian movement, which incorporates and amalgamates various Indian traditions.

Canadian society in general has adopted a system of cultural pluralism in which various groups can maintain their own identity as long as the essential aspects of Anglo-Saxon culture are respected. Vogt states that:

6. *Ibid.*, p. 9.
7. *Ibid.*, p. 12.

Pan-Indianism is assuming a form in which an increasing number of Indians are participating in customs and institutions that are describable only as Indian. These customs and institutions are being synthesized from elements derived from diverse Indian cultures and to some extent from white American culture.[8]

This movement can be seen in the formal and informal groups of Native Peoples who have joined forces to participate in native activities at various Canadian centres. Examples of Pan-Indianism are the native celebrations—such as the Banff Indian Day, the Calgary Stampede, and various powwows—which are organized by the Native Peoples themselves, as well as festivals organized by non-Indians. In all instances, there appears to be enthusiastic inter-band or inter-tribal participation on the part of the Native Peoples, and in the last five years, it seems that Pan-Indianism has developed to the point where it is now an accepted aspect of native organization.

As Vogt has stated, Pan-Indianism contains a variety of cultural elements from diverse segments of the native population:

It is highly significant that a high proportion of these elements are drawn from Plains' culture: war bonnet, the Plains-type war dance, and so on. These elements have become symbols of Indianism to the Indians themselves, to a degree that there is little relationship to the aboriginal facts. . . .

It is probable that their importance as symbols derives in part from the fact that these elements are central features of the prevailing white-American stereotype of the American Indian. They are the features of Indian culture which white tourists expect to find when they attend inter-tribal ceremonials, and Indians are rewarded by the whites for behaving in conformity to the stereotype.[9]

In many areas across North America, one frequently sees rain dances and other tribal celebrations performed by Native Peoples who have no traditional connection with these cultural

8. *Ibid.*
9. *Ibid.*

forms. These festivities indicate how Pan-Indianism has become
a bastardization of various elements of native cultures, but as
Vogt says:

> ... *it has a positive value for it acts as a social and cultural
> framework within which acculturating Indian groups can
> maintain their sense of identity and integrity as long as the
> dominant larger culture assigns them to subordinate status.*[10]

The Pan-Indian movement has been one of the major forces in
the development of the native political, economic, and social
groups that are beginning to speak more effectively for the
increasingly better-organized Canadian Native Peoples. Various
parts of the native population, such as the groups headed by
Walter Currie and Harold Cardinal, are beginning to make their
impact felt on Canadian society. The inevitable outcome of
the frustration experienced by Native Peoples has been the
emergence of the Red Power movement, which will be discussed in more detail in a subsequent chapter.

The question of acculturation cannot be separated from the
process of education. As Zentner states, educational opportunities often depend on the Native Peoples' status in society:

> *Indians may be well or poorly equipped for education in
> Canadian schools depending on how well their culture
> matches that of the society around them.*[11]

Studies such as Nagler's and Hawthorn's[12] have illustrated
the fact that Native Peoples living in large urban centres are, in
some instances, ill-equipped to take advantage of educational
opportunities. By white standards it appears that native children have little motivation for educational achievement—as
their culture has been based on co-operation rather than the

---

10. *Ibid.*, p. 13.
11. H. Zentner, "Parental Behaviour and Student Attitudes towards High
School Graduation, among Indian and Non-Indian Students in Oregon and
Alberta," *Alberta Journal of Education*, Vol. 4, p. 8.
12. M. Nagler, *Indians in the City, op cit.*; and H. Hawthorn, *A Survey of
Contemporary Indians of Canada*, Ottawa: Queen's Printer, 1967.

competition that is the basis of our educational structure. Thus, in communities where both Native Peoples and whites attend the same school, the majority of non-Indian students generally attain higher academic levels than do their native counterparts. Zentner considers that Indian children have "the same mental equipment as their white counterparts, but their cultural status and experience has caused them to rank lower on educational achievement tests."[13] The same results and conclusions have been reached in studies where differences between black and white achievement levels in American schools have been assessed.

If one examines the acculturation processes of various minorities in our society, it is evident that Canadian Indians have not taken part in our educational system at the secondary or higher levels to the same extent as have European immigrants. It appears that many of the native groups have clung to their traditional cultures in ways that have prevented them from adopting the white Canadian culture, including the attitude that education is a means to social mobility and occupational achievement.

According to Havighurst,

> ... those Indian groups who move into the stream of dominant American culture will gradually make more use of schooling and will perform better as scholars. This may take a long time. It seems that Indian groups who do move into the American culture do so at the lower economic level and require a generation or two to learn the ways of upward mobility, including the use of education for this purpose.
>
> Individual Indians have done very well in the American educational system by committing themselves to learning the dominant culture and living in it. The number of such people is relatively small and gives evidence of the great holding power of many of the traditional Indian cultures upon their members, even in the face of pressure and temptation to seek the advantages of the American culture.[14]

13. Zentner, *op. cit.*
14. R. Havighurst, "Education Among American Indians: Individual and Cultural Aspects," *Academy of Political and Social Sciences,* 8, No. 2, May, 1967, p. 150.

In looking at the process of the Native Peoples' education and acculturation in contemporary society, we are really examining one aspect of a larger question, namely, that of the integration of minority groups into the North American social system. In their article, "Integration of Americans of Indian Descent," Dozier, Simpson, and Yinger maintain that two conclusions can be drawn with respect to the assimilation and integration of Canadian Native Peoples.[15] In the first place, communities of Canadian Native Peoples living on reserves will continue to be distinct social units maintaining what has traditionally been defined as their own value system. Their second point implies that Indians on reserves or in communities isolated from Canadian society will resist assimilation although they will constantly make adjustments to the life around them. It is not uncommon to see Native Peoples in these residential centres adopting some aspects of the outside material culture and rejecting others.

Dozier, Simpson, and Yinger postulate, however, that Indian cultures, as distinct, self-contained systems, will eventually disappear. In fact, as the authors point out, many of the Native Peoples have chosen to try to live in both worlds, while others have opted for a traditional way of life, and still others have already rejected their ancestral patterns of existence for a life in Canadian society. The article maintains that optional assimilation on an individual basis, unlike forced assimilation, would leave the way open for the people to adopt Western culture as they themselves desire. The fact is that many Native Peoples continue to live in separate communities and to preserve their traditional cultural life patterns.

It is not the intention of this author to assert that assimilation with the Western ways of life is a desirable end which Indians as a whole should necessarily seek. Many of the Native Peoples as a consequence of their education, of their perception of whites and Western society, and of their isolation from and negative attitude towards that society inevitably choose to live in their own isolated enclaves. For them this existence appears to be most desirable. Their choice of environment is based on a variety of specific associations and attitudes formulated in contact with both native and white society.

---

15. Dozier, Simpson, and Yinger, *op cit.*

In any case, one cannot deny that the ambivalent pressures to which the Native Peoples are subjected have influenced them on the one hand to adopt Western patterns of behaviour, and on the other hand to maintain their traditional patterns of existence. The Native Peoples in many instances are accused of preserving their own value systems *in spite of* opportunities to assimilate, but their value systems—the remnants of their aboriginal cultures — are a result of their socialization and isolation, and their patterns of behaviour and values make sense for any group that lives a tribal existence. These traditions, values, and understandings are not uniquely Indian; they are apparent among any group that lives in a tribal system and is primarily dependent on the physical environment. The same values and cultural practices that have been described as specific to the Indians can be found among tribes of the Amazon, Africa, and Asia, and are typical of any tribal people who have chosen not to assimilate or else who have not had the chance to adopt the patterns inherent in modern industrialized society.

Many tribal societies have derived from the aboriginal social and economic atmosphere a system of obligations dictating that mutual aid be given freely without expectation of return in money or in kind. Aid requested among and between Native Peoples, especially those on reserves or in rural areas, is expected as a matter of right, and will be freely returned. This obligation system works well in these areas, but such expectations are not automatically met in the same way in urban environments. In industrialized urban society, the majority of the Native Peoples feel they must look after their own needs first as they are isolated from their own society. If they have spare time and resources, they may be able to help their fellow Indians, but the expectation of mutual aid is seldom realized among Native Peoples in cities. A Torontorian of Indian ancestry commented:

I have been living in Toronto for a long time and I have had this job for fifteen years. I make good money and live well. Unfortunately I do not have many Indian friends. This is because of lots of reasons. I came here and I did well. My friends from the north heard I had been successful and they began coming to Toronto and the first thing they would do would be to come and see me. They would expect money, room and food. They also expected that I could find jobs for them. My money is enough but especially in the early years, I had to be careful because I had a wife and family. I discovered that my only alternative if I desired to remain here in the city was to keep away from those people. If you can't help all of them, it is not fair to help one or two and my family is the most important. I know for a fact that when Indians enter town, they try and expect to obtain help from their city friends. Most city friends soon discover that here in the city you cannot look after everybody. Because we can't, we don't. We become white men to our former Indian friends.

The system of free mutual aid which is obligatory in most reserve situations cannot for the most part be adapted to an urban environment. Native Peoples who are in a position to sustain themselves independently in the city seldom have the resources to provide for their acquaintances. By not behaving as they would be expected to on a reserve, urban Indians are frequently accused of creating hostility between themselves and their reserve compatriots. This causes real cultural conflict.

Wealth as a symbol of prestige and the success that frequently motivates members of white society to work hard do not appear to be important to most Indians, especially those who are only recently acquainted with urban ways of life. An Indian from northwestern Ontario commented:

I wanted to buy a car there but it is even hard to walk on the road sometimes at home. I really do not know why people want lots of money. At home, we have what we want but we work and if I have a radio or T.V., it is no good because you can't hear it up there. We share everything, because that is the way we live. You people here do not like each other. So I like to have a good time in a nice room. All these things don't cost very much. I guess you see that no one ever steals from an Indian but you see white men down here in the Queen and Spadina district in Toronto having money stolen. If you don't have nothing, nobody can steal. Have you ever heard of anybody stealing from an Indian?[16]

16. Nagler, research notes from *Indians in the City, op cit.*

To many Native Peoples, especially to those who have always lived in rural areas and on reserves, saving money in the sense generally accepted in North American society is meaningless. In rural areas, saving on an individual basis is considered selfish and irresponsible because it contravenes the expectations of mutual aid. Economic acquisitiveness, saving, and placing a high value on goods or monetary resources are not prevalent, since sharing is considered a means of providing and hence is taken as a matter of course. Hoarding negates the normative pattern of sharing and would inevitably lead to the alienation of the hoarder. In traditional environments, the Native Peoples found that large quantities of goods, such as game, cannot always be used or kept by one person and hence group co-operation was necessary. Saving for future well-being, or delay of gratification for future benefit, is not a logical pattern of behaviour for Native Peoples.

Except for those who live in cities or are familiar with Western patterns of life, Native Peoples seldom if ever consider depositing their money in banks or investing their funds. Many of them appear to have little concern for future exigencies and, as a result, they spend their money as soon as possible and rarely in a manner that those in white society would consider prudent. As one Indian said:

> I fly to Sioux Lookout three or four times a year. I make lots of money from the American tourists. But money is no good up there so I come in to the Sioux or Toronto to have a good time. Now I can get a haircut. At one time, they would not cut your hair if you were an Indian. I spend all the money. There is not too much to buy in the way of supplies because we make most of our own stuff. A lot of the boys fly back and forth. You say we should save money. What for?

Another Indian commented:

> I finally had enough money to buy a car. I had it for two years and I spent all of my money on it. I would like to go back to school, but I spend all my money that I have on riding around. I pump gas anyway and that is good enough.[17]

17. Interviews taken in Kenora by the author.

Another cultural pattern generally attributed to the Native Peoples is their concept of time. It has often been said that Indians cannot adapt to the time requirements of white society. For natives attuned to life in a traditional physical environment, time generally is geared to seasonal variations. In this rural context, the Native Peoples, by and large, are not dependent on the white men's social and economic systems, and their behaviour is suited to the contingencies of their traditional living patterns. The accusation that Native Peoples are frequently not dependable is illustrated by the following interview recorded in Red River:

Yes I lost my job. I was supposed to be there at eight o'clock every morning. I never had to get up that early back home. At home you do something that has to be done, but you do it differently. In some weeks you gather supplies. At other times you must go to town. But it doesn't make any problems, whether you go to work at eight o'clock in the morning or at two o'clock in the afternoon, or the next day.

On the reserve, clock time serves no important purpose in terms of present or future needs and obligations. Agricultural and hunting activities are organized according to seasonal variations, but other activities need not be organized at definite times because they fulfil no immediate needs. Edward Rogers maintains that the Indians' concept of time is totally different from that of the white society's but just as valid and better suited both to the way of life that they pursued in the past and to their present way of functioning. Native Peoples always will perform tasks that they perceive as necessary, but without reference to a specific time. As Rogers maintains:

The Indian system of life dictated, and still dictates, in some reserve areas, today, that they act according to circumstances rather than a particular predefined time. The Indian does not value time as we do—certainly not his own time. It has no dollar value.[18]

18. E. S. Rogers, "Indian Time," *Ontario Fish and Wildlife Review*, 4, No. 4, 1965, pp. 23-26.

This lack of appreciation of the monetary value of time is well illustrated by the incident related by the manager of a television appliance shop in a northern community:

I have had four Indians working for me in the last three years. These boys unlike many of my other workers were not very communicative. They were strong and good workers when they worked. That is the problem. Some of them just do not ever come in on time and one fellow did not show up for three weeks, and then he came here one day expecting to work. I cannot take him back. I operate a business. They just do not feel an obligation to work as the company works. I have had this problem before.

The concept of time is essentially a cultural value and therefore means one thing to a traditionally oriented person of Indian descent and another thing to Euro-Canadians. It is this difference that is perhaps one of the major reasons why many people of native descent have difficulty in adapting to the urban way of life. When an Indian is required to adapt to white time values, he frequently cannot adjust to the demands made on him—as he is bound to his sense of time in the same way that whites are bound to theirs. Thus when the North American native is criticized as unreliable and unable to hold a job, it must be remembered that he never had to think in terms of "another day, another dollar." The work ethic among traditionally oriented Native Peoples is at variance with the established urban pattern of existence. Reserve-influenced natives think more in terms of group welfare than individual well-being. Their planning for the future is defined in terms of seasons and in terms of what should be done so that all may thrive according to the best attainable standards.

It appears that these normative patterns or values are universal among native groups. Indians who enter Western society and who want to participate in that society must discard their native values and incorporate at least some of those of the host society. Living in Western society and being a part of it may not be a positive goal for many of the Indians who value the traditional patterns of life that can still be preserved and maintained in rural environments. The older members of native society, as in other minority groups, tend to shun many of the modern Western ways and consider them potentially corruptive and disruptive. Thus many sectors of the native population are caught in the dilemma of whether or not to opt for the "society out there," or pay heed to the advice and direction of their elders. If they listen to the warnings of their elders, they will approach most white institutions with distrust. One example of this distrust is the natives' attitudes towards Western education, which will be discussed in the following chapter.

3 Education

The educational system is one of the most important areas where Native Peoples have come into contact with the rest of North American society. However, Indians have not fared well. Until the present time, the majority of Indians on reserves were educated with books and other material that seldom related to their own culture, but rather reflected that of middle-class Canadian society. Partly as a result of this, the majority of the Native Peoples did not remain in school any longer than legally required. Prior to 1967 the government tried in many parts of Canada to enroll reserve Indians in residential schools. The Native Peoples objected to the fact that their families were split up (the residential schools were often located far away from the reserves) and that what was being taught was of little relevance to their way of life. The schools were not successful and have since been abandoned.

The above situation was compounded by the fact that many teachers in these schools had little knowledge of or previous contact with Native Peoples. The teachers were often of second-rate calibre as well. (Most of the highly qualified teachers opted to teach in larger urban centres where students were more receptive and where modern educational facilities were available.) Consequently, many of the native pupils did not become interested or involved enough in their studies to go on to higher levels of education. Data collected in 1972 by Ernest McEwan, former executive director of the Indian-Eskimo Association of

Canada, substantiate this point.[1] The data show that 50 per cent of the native population do not advance beyond the sixth grade, 61 per cent do not complete grade eight, and 97 per cent do not graduate from high school (See Table 1).

TABLE 1

Progress of Indian Students Through a Twelve-Year School Cycle, 1972[a]

GRADE	YEAR	ENROLLMENT	LOSS (#)	LOSS (%)
1	1951	8782	——	——
2	1952	4544	4238	48.2
3	1953	3930	614	13.5
4	1954	3652	278	7.1
5	1955	3088	564	15.5
6	1956	2641	447	19.5
7	1957	2090	551	21.7
8	1958	1536	559	26.5
9	1959	1149	387	25.5
10	1960	730	419	36.5
11	1961	482	248	34.0
12	1962	341	141	29.3

[a] E.R. McEwan *Report of the Executive Director*, Indian-Eskimo Association of Canada, June, 1972, p. 78..

Professor Andre Renaud, in his paper "Education from Within,"[2] cites various factors needed to educate any minority group successfully. The successful teacher should know the psychology of his pupils and the type of knowledge and skills that they bring to the classroom. He should also be familiar with the most advanced methods, procedures, resources, and measuring instruments available so that he can encourage students to make the best possible use of the abilities they have learned from their cultural environment. The teacher must therefore not only be an educator but also a quasi social engineer. But, in reality, most schools in which there are native students are staffed by teachers who are seldom fully aware of the special difficulties the children face, nor of the fact that, although the majority of Indians accept that education will

1. E. R. McEwan, *Report of the Executive Director*, Indian-Eskimo Association of Canada, June, 1972.
2. A. Renaud, "Education from Within," unpublished manuscript.

improve their lot in society, many of them are apprehensive about losing their culture and institutions.

In May, 1973, the Indian Affairs Branch issued a memorandum proposing that local areas be given authority over education. The government and some of the Native Peoples hope that this policy will help to involve Indians in their own educational process and encourage conditions in which the Indians will be able to view education as a means of achieving mobility within Canadian society.

Prior to 1950, government policy neglected the education of the Native Peoples, which was handled by various religious organizations. In some instances, missionary-run schools were able to educate small groups of the native population successfully, but as Harold Cardinal maintains:

> *Unfortunately much more has to be said about the role the misguided missionaries played in the disruption of the Indians' way of life and their direct responsibility for the failure of Indians to achieve educational parity with non-Indian society . . . .*
>
> *The unvarnished truth is that the missionaries of all Christian sects regarded the Indians as savages, heathens or something worse. They made no attempt to understand Indian religious beliefs, virtually no attempt to appreciate Indian cultural values and paid little heed to Indian ways. The true purpose of the schools they established was to process good little Christian boys and girls —but only Christians of the sect operating the school. In those early church schools, academic knowledge occupied one of the back seats. Since the Indian was expected to live in isolation from the rest of society, obviously all the education he needed was a bit of reading, writing, figures and some notion of hygiene.*[3]

Perhaps education was a secondary goal of the missionary schools, since the missionaries often were more interested in converting the Indians than in educating them. The arrangement was convenient for the government because it kept "the savages quiet."[4] The Indians were further disillusioned by edu-

---

3. H. Cardinal, *The Unjust Society*, Edmonton: Hurtig, 1970, pp. 35, 53.
4. *Ibid.*, p. 53.

cation because they could see how different denominations were struggling to capture Indian souls for their own group. By and large, the standards of education were exceptionally low. Few of the teachers were acquainted with the native languages, customs, and cultures, and the majority were completely unconcerned with the preservation and growth of traditional native ways of life. The missionary schools caused much dissent when they became residential because they tended to break up native families. With their emphasis on the dominant culture and their disregard for the native cultures, these residential schools alienated native children from the educational process, from religion and from their families. The students often had their values confused; one native now living in Toronto stated that he had been physically punished whenever he was caught speaking his native language with fellow students at his residential school in Brantford.

The residential educational system was abandoned in the mid-sixties when the federal government opted for non-denominational education. Until May, 1973, however, the government maintained its policy of not including the Native Peoples in the educational curricula designed for white children. Now Indian students in some areas are educated in the same schools as their non-Indian counterparts, and although it is difficult to assess completely the effect of this program, needless to say the native children are at a severe disadvantage because their social environment has not provided them with the abilities and tools to function successfully in this type of learning environment. Hawthorn's report on Indians in Canada states:

> It is the policy of the department to educate Indian children wherever possible in association with other children, particularly where accommodation is available and practical in a provincial school system and provided the Indians approve. The last phrase—"provided the Indians approve"—may be allowed in theory, but in practice it hasn't worked that way. No one bothers to ask the Indians.[5]

5. Hawthorn, op. cit., p. 56.

In a reversal of former policies it appears that the government now is trying to encourage the preservation of native cultures within the educational system. Canada has become more conscious of its ethnic minorities since the late Prime Minister Pearson established the Bilingualism and Biculturalism Commission in the early sixties. The Commission focused on the nature and condition of the two major cultures in Canada, but it also pointed out the value of diverse cultures and identities in the Canadian mosaic. Many of the Native Peoples are not satisfied with the theoretical perspectives of the Commission because they believe it ignored their cultures. However, the Commission did heighten awareness of the Quebec fact in Canada, and this in turn helped to promote the concept of a culturally pluralistic society in which all minorities should be encouraged to maintain their cultural heritage. As Cardinal observed:

> *If changes are not made (in the educational system), and soon; if the control of education continues to be outside the sphere of the Indian people, the future of our people looks truly bleak.*[6]

One of the major difficulties in changing the educational system for Indians, as for others, is that of defining what is or should be meant by education. Obviously, education is a means of conveying the values, goals, and practices of a society to the young in order to equip them to participate effectively in that society. The difficulty, as Renaud points out, is that societies differ in their beliefs and images and, therefore, patterns of instruction must take different forms according to the society involved. As Renaud maintains:

> *Today, children of Indian descent are being schooled presumably for competence in our society rather than for what is left of their own, and therein lies the difficulty. As much as possible, because of this overall objective, Indian children for the last 25 years have been offered an identical schooling process to the one offered to other children in the country. A*

6. Cardinal, *op. cit.*, p. 61.

cursory look at the results described in the statistics not only
of school promotion but of human experience on the reserves
is enough to conclude that this approach has so far produced
rather poor results .... [7]

According to Renaud, the Canadian identity is much more confused and diffused than it was in earlier times, or in other
societies. He describes Canadian society as a talking, literate,
scientific, urban, multi-cultural, multi-ethnic, industrialized
society that is commercialized around a value system based on
the use of money and extolling private property and marketable
skills.[8]

In contrast, Renaud points out that Indian communities are
more homogeneous, and are based on a totally different value
system. In the first place, he finds that native communities are
characterized by a "continuation of a silent type of human society, as oral communication does not play the role in native
society that it has traditionally played in our society."[9] Indian
society can function adequately without the benefit of full liter-
acy, as it is pre-scientific and traditionally oriented. Hence, the
patterns of socialization and values that the Indians teach their
children reflect the norms of the society of which they are a part.
Renaud maintains that the reserve system produced homogeneous communities and the "cross-fertilization of ideas, skills, and
attitudes is still kept to a minimum, and inbreeding is
constant."[10] Native communities are still not part of industrialized society, since their output in terms of goods and services tends to be limited to their own needs. These societies "do
not fully operate on the dollar system,"[11] and all services, including government aid, come without a price tag. In addition,
most Indian communities have less than a thousand members
and therefore tend to maintain *Gemeinschaft* relationships because of the social and psychological repercussions of their
geographical separation. This separateness, according to Renaud, has the effect of producing a closely knit in-group as

7. Renaud, *op. cit.*, p. 3
8. *Ibid.*, p. 4
9. *Ibid.*, p. 5.
10. *Ibid.*, p. 9.
11. *Ibid.*, p. 10.

opposed to the outside world and a lack of awareness that there could be mutually beneficial co-operation between the two. As Renaud states, "this is a very poor basis for integration of any kind,"[12] and creates a cultural gap which is difficult, if not impossible, to bridge by the traditional educational patterns.

It must be remembered, however, that the various Indian tribes across North America have always been successful in educating their children according to their own traditional ways.[13] They have done so mainly by example, rather than by a formal educational process that is separated from their daily life. The difficulty with North American education, so far as the Native Peoples are concerned, is that the education they have received from this society has been directed at inculcating them with Canadian culture in the hope of Canadianizing them. As Renaud's discussion illustrates, this is a new and different culture to that of the Native Peoples and the traditional three R's of our system have nothing to do with their family-life patterns, religions, and traditional tribal processes. As Havighurst wrote,

> . . . the Indian who is subjected to white education becomes a man of two cultures. Sometimes the Indian culture predominates and sometimes the white culture wins. Generally the individual makes his own combination of the two by adopting such white "ways" as are useful and pleasant to him including farming and homemaking skills, artisan skills and often a form of Christianity.[14]

Havighurst concurs with Renaud in pointing out that native cultures do not equip Indian children for education in Canadian schools and that the children's success in the school system therefore depends on how well their culture matches that of the Canadian industrial society around them. One would expect that Indians who are subject to strong urban influences would achieve greater success in education. Indeed, the data collected for *Indians in the City* indicate that Native Peoples who are educated in urban areas, or in areas subject to urban influences,

12. *Ibid.*
13. Havighurst, *op. cit.*
14. *Ibid.*, p. 92.

are more likely to accommodate themselves to the goals of Canadian society.[15] However, there is also an exceptionally high drop-out rate among those of native descent in urban areas. One can postulate that cultural backgrounds, prejudice and discrimination, and many native students' feeling that they are foreigners in the classroom contribute to this drop-out rate.

One might expect that most Indians living close to urban communities would be motivated towards competitive achievement and would be economically better off than those from rural areas. Indeed, one might hypothesize an order of native communities ranked in terms of the type and size of white communities to which they have easiest access. Hawthorn's data illustrate that in many instances Indians from isolated rural areas have low levels of consumer aspirations and low economic standards, and that some of the most economically developed bands are located near larger metropolitan concentrations. However, his findings were not entirely consistent for he also found that some of the most depressed Indian bands were living in or near prosperous and expanding business or industrial centres that would seem to offer a multitude of job opportunities. Hence Hawthorn's data suggest that in fact there may be little correlation between urban proximity, education, and economic opportunity.

Oscar Lewis, like other prominent anthropologists and sociologists, has applied the concept of the culture of poverty to the poor of many groups of ethnic origin living in highly industrialized areas. Lewis estimates that at least 20 per cent of the poor exhibit characteristics quantitively different from those found among the majority of middle-class North Americans:

> *This culture of poverty is characterized by a low level of organization. It is not integrated with the major institutions of society, contains a deep-rooted hostility towards representatives of the larger society — for example social workers, politicians and police, and persons within the culture possess feelings of hopelessness, dependence and inferiority.*[16]

15. Nagler, *Indians in the City*, op. cit.
16. J. Harp and J. R. Hofley, eds., *Poverty in Canada*, Scarborough, Ont.: Prentice-Hall of Canada, 1971, p. 219.

These are, in many cases, the same factors that have prevented a large proportion of the Native Peoples from attaining the standards of education and the patterns of living that are the ideals of Western society.

It appears that it is not ethnic or economic background as such that creates educational difficulties, but the differences between the values of the educational system and those values the students grew up with. As Harp and Hofley maintain, the extent to which one culture can be integrated with another depends, "not primarily on individual good or ill-will, but on social values and attitudes and on institutions to mediate the induction of alien individuals into it. "[17] The difficulties that the Native Peoples have had in participating fully in the Canadian educational system stem largely from the fact that they are not ready to integrate culturally with the larger society, and that that society is not receptive to what are considered socially and culturally alien peoples. Although theoretically the long-term goal of education in our society is integration, in practice neither those who are to be integrated nor the society into which they are to be inculcated are receptive enough to achieve this end.

As discussed in Chapter 2, theorists at one time maintained that an educational system allowing acculturation would inevitably bring about social integration among the diverse groups in North America and that the minorities would eventually become "typical North Americans."[18] That ideal has not been realized and theorists now are emphasizing cultural pluralism and extolling the virtues of individuality with co-operation among diverse groups. Most of Canada's minority groups in fact have been able to assimilate the patterns of Canadian culture while maintaining many of their unique cultural characteristics — but this has not been the case with the Native Peoples. One reason for this is that they have not, until recently, had the same educational opportunities as the children of most immigrant groups, and it is mainly through education that the second-generation immigrants have been integrated in Canadian cultural traditions.

17. *Ibid.*
18. Hallowell, *op. cit.*, p. 215.

Outside of the family, educational institutions are the most effective way to convey the generally acknowledged values, mores, folkways, and laws that define and perpetuate contemporary society. For the most part in Canada, these institutions have refrained from transgressing on the cultural traditions valued by particular minorities. But because the Native Peoples, with some justification, have viewed education as a one-way process involving "foreign" techniques and consisting of subjects that rarely have any relevance to their way of life, they have not been able to take advantage even of the limited educational opportunities offered them. Recently several native groups have criticized many aspects of contemporary education, but their protocts have reflected individualized rather than group interests, and have therefore had little effect. At present, more interest is being shown in training teachers specifically to teach Native Peoples, using materials that Indian children can recognize as part of their daily lives. Also, more Native Peoples are themselves training to become teachers and are returning to teach in their communities. Hopefully the gap between what is taught in the schools and what is learned in the community will lessen and Native Peoples will through education retain their own culture while absorbing what of Western culture will be of advantage to them.

4 Legal Status, Intermarriage, and Religion

The reserve system served to isolate the Native Peoples physically, psychologically, and socially from the mainstream of contemporary society. As a consequence of the *Indian Act* they are now the only minority group legally distinguished from other Canadians. The effect of this legal distinction on the important factors of intermarriage and religion will be examined to demonstrate how early contacts with Europeans have continued to influence the attitudes of the Native Peoples. Intermarriage, once sanctioned by tribal traditions, is still uncommon. The Native Peoples, influenced in many instances by their traditional religious beliefs and practices, have seldom been solid converts to the religions of Western man. But their contact with Western society has had a considerable and changing influence on the pattern of intermarriage and on the pattern of religious observances now current among those of native descent. In the first instance it is necessary to briefly examine the Native Peoples' legal status. Initially their legal status through the *Indian Act* was designed to protect them and to permit them to participate more effectively with Canadian society. In fact, the *Indian Act* for the most part increased the isolation of Native Peoples from the mainstream of Canadian society.

In Canada, most tribal cultures were built on small units and tended to be based on primary relationships. In this *Gemeinschaft* society, the Indians' legal status and roles were defined by tradition. Fishing, hunting, and gathering supplied their material needs; the output of a tribal group was sufficient only for its own use, with perhaps a little surplus for bartering. The arrival of the white man created vast markets for native goods, particularly furs. These initial contacts were generally positive, because the Indians benefited from the trading and at the same time the Europeans learned bush survival from the Native Peoples. The relationship changed rapidly, however: by the seventeenth century, the Native Peoples were being subjugated by the Europeans.

A large number of the Native Peoples, in providing for the demands of the Europeans, divorced themselves from their traditions and in doing so disrupted their patterns of life socially, economically, psychologically, and politically. As in the United States, the Native Peoples of Canada gradually were separated from white society and put into enclaves known as reserves or reservations. These reserves were intended to be areas in which the Native Peoples could maintain their traditional ways of life, but subsequent developments have shown that the reserve system served to break down these traditional patterns. The reserve system, together with the rights and status of Native Peoples, was established as law when the first *Indian Act* was passed in 1876.

Canadian Indians are the only minority in Canada whose legal rights are prescribed in an act of Parliament. The *Indian Act* defines what a legal Indian is and what constitutes his rights and obligations concerning matters of property, residence, possession of lands, sale of goods, inheritance, guardianship, management of "Indian monies," political administration by the government and by the Indians themselves, and processes of enfranchisement. Although over the years the *Act* has been debated, reviewed and in many instances changed, it continues to be a source of frustration to the Indians.

Present government policies have been directed towards enabling the Indians to become full Canadian citizens. In a speech in Vancouver in 1969, Prime Minister Trudeau said: "The Indians should become Canadians as have all other Canadians." Although some of the Native Peoples agree, many more maintain that such a policy instituted on behalf of the Native Peoples would lead to cultural genocide. In order to maintain their identity, the Indians are now agitating for guarantees of the aboriginal rights granted to them under treaty. Treaties had been made with individual Indian tribes during the process of colonization in order to protect them and allow them to live according to their traditional lifestyles. According to Harold Cardinal:

> *These treaties represent an Indian magna carta. . . . We entered into these negotiations with faith, with hope for a better life with honour. . . . Did the white man enter into them with something less in mind? Or have the heirs of the men who signed in honour somehow disavowed the obligation passed down to them?*[1]

Policies formulated by government officials after 1969 seem to be based on the premise that the *Indian Act* should be abrogated. The position of the Indians who oppose this view is dramatically pointed out by Cardinal:

> *As far as we are concerned, our treaty rights represent a sacred honourable agreement between ourselves and the Canadian government that cannot be unilaterally abrogated by the government at the whim of one of its leaders, unless the government is prepared to give us back title to our country. . . . We cannot give up our rights without destroying ourselves.*[2]

The Native Peoples are concerned about keeping their traditional rights of fishing, trapping, and hunting. They are concerned about keeping the rights of education, land, and health services they were guaranteed by the Queen. Cardinal goes on to maintain that the Indian People must distrust the agreements of the white men:

> *The Indian People cannot be blamed for feeling that not until the sun ceases to shine, the rivers cease to flow, and the grasses to grow, or wonder of wonders, the government decides to honour its treaties, will the white men cease to speak with forked tongues.*[3]

1. Cardinal, *op. cit.*, p. 28.
2. *Ibid.*, p. 30.
3. *Ibid.*, p. 38.

The Indians were led to believe by the treaties and by the *Indian Act* that they were entitled to free education and free medical aid, among other considerations. There has been disagreement as to what was meant by these guarantees, for the Native Peoples believe that the government as signatory to the treaties symbolized government commitment to Indian rights and protection. The *Indian Act* was subsequently passed in order to implement the terms of the treaties, but according to Cardinal the *Act*, rather than protecting native rights, "subjugated to colonial rule the very people it was supposed to protect."[4] Some of the sections of the *Act* certainly support this contention. For example, Section 18 maintains that the Minister may authorize the use of the reserves, or sections of them, for any purpose that he deems necessary. Section 35 states that local authorities may take land for any purposes with the consent of the Governor in Council. Section 45, Part 3, in regard to native wills, lays down that:

> No will executed by an Indian is of any legal force or effect as the disposition of property until the minister has approved the will, or has granted probate thereof pursuant of this will.[5]

Section 46 lists a number of ways whereby the Minister may declare a will null and void such as if "the terms of the will are against public interest."[6] The *Act* also authorized control of Indian monies by the Minister, and control over construction of any buildings on Indian lands.

Admittedly, the Native Peoples have been given some benefits according to the *Act* (they are not taxed for monies earned on the reserve for example) but the number of prohibitions greatly outweighs the number of benefits. The *Act* lays down severe penalties for truancy among those of school age, and states that an Indian child who "refuses or fails to attend school regularly shall be deemed to be a juvenile delinquent within the meaning of the *Juvenile Delinquent Act*."[7] Further examination of the

4. *Ibid.*, p. 44.
5. *Indian Act*, R.S.C. 1952, C149 as ammended by 1960-61, Department of Citizenship and Immigration, Ottawa.
6. *Ibid.*
7. *Ibid.*

Indian Act reveals many more provisions which appear not so much to protect the Indian as to reduce him to a manipulated member of a minority group. In most of the legislation affecting native rights, the Indians themselves have seldom if ever been consulted, with the inevitable long-term result that government legislation and negotiations, insofar as the majority of the Native Peoples are concerned, have alienated them from the government and from Canadian society.

Many Native Peoples who are aware of the negative aspects of the mandates between themselves and the Queen have lobbied for the abolition of federal control of Indian affairs, and many provinces, Quebec included, have started to develop policies in the belief that Indian affairs will eventually come under provincial authority. Other Native Peoples, especially those in Quebec, have expressed the wish to remain under the federal government, as opposed to provincial administrations which they fear are more likely to be hostile to their interests. The fact remains that, because of their past experience, the Native Peoples do not expect that legislation concerning them will be equitable or consistent no matter where the ultimate authority lies. Currently justifying this point of view is the James Bay development program, which the natives believe is not legal because of guarantees given to them in the last century. The more realistic element of native society points out that the interests of the dominant society will always take precedence over the interests of Indians in any policy decision, and that the Native Peoples can do little to affect such decisions. The Native Peoples themselves are seldom in agreement as to what policies would in the long run be most beneficial to their welfare, but when they do agree, it appears that even their concerted efforts cannot sway government sympathies towards their needs. The apparent readiness of the Quebec government to proceed with the James Bay development is a case in point.

Arguments have been advanced by the Native Peoples that the government should change its policy with regard to them. In the United States, federal supervision over some of the tribes has already been terminated and in Canada there are some who advocate that the federal government should adopt a similar policy. There are, however, opponents who argue that many

Indians are not prepared to enter white society and neither is that society prepared to receive them; that Indians could not as yet compete on an equal basis with long-established industrial corporations. Although many Indians are against the forced assimilation that would result from termination of government control of the reserves, they believe that the Native Peoples will gradually adjust to white society while retaining something of their own cultures, and that "optional assimilation on an individual basis, unlike forced assimilation, would leave the way open for assimilation to occur 'at the speed and in the direction which the people themselves desire'."[8]

The Indians have tended to resent the government's paternalistic attitudes, and to distrust the white men because of the many times treaties have been broken and legislation relating to Indian affairs has been changed without consultation with Native Peoples. As with many minority groups, distrust of the larger society has led to ghettoization. This in turn leads to further feelings of social inferiority, because the relationship between white society and the minority groups are governed by laws, attitudes, and values of the larger society which the minority can neither sympathize with nor aspire to attain.

Since the time of the earliest European settlement, contacts between the two groups have been influenced by racial differences, legal and social pressures, and cultural norms that defined appropriate behaviour in white terms. One of the areas in which these factors have had considerable influence is that of legal and non-legal marital patterns between whites and Indians. Like other North American minorities, the Native Peoples tend to disapprove of intermarriage because they see it as a step that in the long run will inhibit rather than promote their participation as equals in North American society.

The Native Peoples, unlike other minorities in the North American framework, have been more or less confined for legal and quasi-legal reasons to reserve environments, and have only recently started to drift away, both physically and socially, from their traditional homes. Even with increasing contacts with the

8. K. and D. French, "The Warm Springs Indian Community," *The American Indian*, 7, No. 2, Spring, 1955, p. 16.

larger society, the incidence of intermarriage has not increased appreciably for a variety of reasons.

Many North American minorities have regarded marriage with members of the majority group as an improvement in social and economic status and as a measure of their acceptance in society. This has never been the case with the Native Peoples, however. The initial contacts between the Native Peoples and the European arrivals did not lead to intermarriage on any large scale and the gap between the two groups has tended to increase rather than lessen. The cultural differences between Native Peoples and European settlers have always been greater than those between most minority immigrant groups, and the physical and social barriers that emerged enhanced, at least from the European perspective, the value of separate identities.

The marriages that did take place between whites and Native Peoples were initially the result of direct social and environmental contacts, and occurred with increasing frequency mainly in areas where there was a shortage of European women. Hence in the years following European immigration, "liaisons" between the Native Peoples and non-Indians followed the pattern of non-Indian men marrying Indian women. However, the prevailing attitudes among both Native Peoples and non-Indians have always deterred large-scale intermarriage. These attitudes are a consequence of the socialization process, stereotypes prevailing in respective social environments, lack of opportunities for contacts, past negative experiences, and peer-group disapproval. As far as the Native Peoples are concerned, sanctions against intermarriage are frequently exercised within traditional environments, but carry little weight when the Indian involved chooses to move away from the reserve.

Recent research data[9] shows that there is still relatively little intermarriage between Indians and whites. Indians born in or close to an urban environment more often intermarry than those who are born and raised in rural, reserve-type environments, however. Traditional Indian practices appear to have little or no influence on the issue of intermarriage, because the majority of

9. M. Nagler, "North American Indians and Intermarriage," *Interracial Marriage,* I.R. Stuart and L.E. Abt, eds., New York: Grossman, 1973, p. 288.

Indians marrying whites come from non-traditional family, educational, and social backgrounds and are more ambivalent about their attitude towards their status as Indians. The majority of those who do intermarry are more likely to be associated with the middle- and upper-income groups in Canadian society, are not firmly attached to Indian traditions, and do not maintain ties with the reserves. It is difficult to speculate with any degree of accuracy on the effect of religion on the Indians who have chosen to intermarry, as those interviewed indicated only marginal religious attachment.

Marriage between the Native Peoples and non-Indians occurs infrequently and takes place in three relatively distinct types of social environments. In the cities, the prevalent pattern is that of educated young Indian men marrying educated non-Indian women with contacts usually made in educational institutions, universities, government offices, etc. In blue-collar environments, intermarriage, although rare, generally occurs in small settlements near areas with a large Indian population. In these areas, white men of educational levels below high school frequently marry Indian women of similar educational background. Intermarriage seldom occurs in this type of social environment because there are usually rigid caste barriers between Indians and whites. In frontier environments, intermarriage usually involves white men and Indian women—generally attributed to the fact that the opportunity for contact between white men and white women is limited in this situation.

Thus it seems that the most common pattern of marriage between Indians and non-Indians involve Native men marrying women of non-native descent. This is because Indian women, except in the frontier situation, have fewer opportunities for meeting men in other groups than Indian men have for meeting non-native women. Also, ethnic, racial, religious, and institutional controls exert a stronger influence on Indian women than on Indian men as far as intermarriage is concerned. For a non-white, marrying a white woman or a woman from a minority group whose appearance and manners closely approximate those of white women is frequently viewed in North American society as a symbol of success and prestige, and as an indication of belonging to the larger community.

As previously pointed out, various sections of the *Indian Act* have deterred Indian women from marrying non-Indians for, when they do, they automatically lose their treaty status and rights. But when women of non-native descent marry Indians, they assume legal Indian status under the treaty. This has been considered by many as a reflection of a masculine bias. The Native Peoples are at present debating whether or not the present policy should be upheld, but the diverse opinions of the various groups make it impossible for them to present a united case to the government. However, small groups or individuals are fighting the present legislation in the courts. Jeannette Corbiere Lavall, an Ojibway woman who married a white man, fought to retain her Indian status before the Supreme Court of Canada. In 1971 the Federal Court ruled that the plaintiff had been legally deprived of her Indian status. As Mrs. Lavall said:

> *Because European men looked upon their own women as something that they owned — they didn't have any rights — they decided that Indian men should do the same. This is very important, that the Indian Act was created from a white point of view.*[10]

In September, 1973 a subsequent decision by the Supreme Court of Canada upheld the ruling that Mrs. Lavall had been legally deprived of her Indian status. Even among the Indian population there was considerable discord about whether or not Mrs. Lavall and other women of native descent should be allowed to retain their Indian status after intermarriage. Those who question Mrs. Lavall's position maintain that, if she had won her case, white men would be allowed on the reserves and hence native culture would be subject to more pressure than it currently encounters.

This fear that their culture is endangered by pressure from whites affects the Native Peoples' attitudes to white intervention in many spheres. A good example of this is their distrust of missionaries and priests. Although Indians have always been

10. G.E. Simpson and J.M. Yinger, *Racial and Cultural Minorities*, New York: Harper Row, 1970, p. 37.

religious people, they have often been disillusioned with Christianity. Missionary activities of the white men have served in many instances to break down the Indians' traditional beliefs. On the West Coast, for example, missionary zeal was often put to the task of burning down native totem poles and destroying other artifacts of religious value to the Native Peoples. In endeavouring to save the Indians from the devil, the efforts the missionaries made to inculcate the Indians with the values, traditions, and beliefs of Christianity proved to be unsuccessful, for the majority of Indians have never adopted Christianity in any deep sense. The Christianity the Indians practise on the reserves tends to be instrumental religion – that is, many of the Native Peoples may go to a Catholic church one day and to a Protestant church on another, because they enjoy participating in the celebrations or religious festivals of either denomination. Although some religious denominations have done beneficial work among the Indians (for example, in education and medicine) their interdenominational rivalry has disillusioned the Indians. As a result, the majority of the Native Peoples regard the white man's religion with the same jaundiced eye as they regard other white institutions. It appears that the younger Native Peoples, even those in metropolitan centres, are returning to traditional native observances, for these are felt to be a valuable part of their culture.

Traditionally, Canadian Indians are a religious people in that they have always maintained deep spiritual feelings and beliefs. Their religions vary considerably in terms of ritual and dogma, but they all are based on the belief that things, animals, trees, and rocks, are inhabited by a spirit that can aid them in times of difficulty. According to Fraser Symington, there were:

... so many deities, great and small, nearly every act was a ritual intended in part to gain help or avoid punishment by some god. All dances were in some degree religious dances. Amulets, charms, medicine bags and various herbs and grasses were part of the equipment of almost every Canadian Indian in his never-ending intercourse with the spirits. Less concrete but no less real in the minds of most Indians were the chants, incantations, personal songs, prayers and rituals

which had essentially the same purpose – to influence the
spirit world toward benevolence.

Many shamans and sorcerers, jugglers and conjurers had
special arsenals of weapons with which they might damage
enemies by occult power, or engage more intimately with the
deities to gain information or to intercede on behalf of a sick
man or to benefit the tribe and damage its enemies. Some of
the mystic paraphernalia could be sold or passed on to sons
and daughters. Some of it went with a man on his final
journey to the spirit world.[11]

The way the Indian peoples conceive of religion is diametri-
cally opposed to many of the teachings of Western Christianity.
The Christian tradition emphasizes the brevity of man's earthly
existence and regards life as a way-station for the hereafter.
Indians, on the other hand, emphasize the present and have
never been unduly concerned about the future life. For them
religion is seen in more utilitarian terms and they therefore
expect help and success in their everyday life. Religious fulfill-
ment is much more materialistic and is shown in such things as
successful hunts, fishing expeditions, harvests, freedom from
sickness, many children, and long lives. These are the blessings
that Indians traditionally seek from their religion.

They realized, nevertheless, that this life also is uncertain,
that no religion could release them from all its trials and
perils, and, like mortals everywhere, they submitted in blind
resignation to the misfortunes that inevitably cross man's
path.[12]

Like many primitive peoples, North American Indians tended
to be polytheistic, but some, such as the Algonkians and the
Iroquoian-Oneida, subscribed to a form of monotheism. These
tribes attributed the mysterious powers or forces operating in
man's environment to the essence of one great spirit. In most

11. F. Symington, *The Canadian Indian*, Toronto: McClelland and Stewart
Limited, 1969, p. 55.
12. D. Jenness, *The Indians of Canada*, Ottawa: Queen's Printer, 1963, p. 167.

tribes, however, bad spirits were thought to be responsible for success or disaster; the Cree, for example, attributed the smallpox outbreak in 1781-82 to the "bad spirit."

Values such as the maintenance of a pollution-free environment have always been of prime importance to the native population for practical as well as religious reasons. The natives of the Pacific Coast attached religious significance to the annual salmon run, and so maintained that it would be a sin in any way to pollute the salmon streams. The Iroquois in many areas of Eastern Canada refuse to allow their dogs to eat beaver bones, for they believed that this would be an insult to the spirit of the beaver and would inhibit if not prevent a successful hunt. Hence, religion was for the Native Peoples a rationalization of their patterns of life.

The revival of traditional native religion is in part a product of some Indians' desire to maintain their aboriginal traditions; it is being encouraged by the increasingly positive self-image that the Native Peoples have. It is also partly a result of the old disillusionment many Indians felt towards Christianity because of the conflict among the various Christian denominations and their concept that many of the rituals and practices in native religions were sinful. The maintenance and revival of interest in native religious observances can thus be seen as a reflection of the changing image and position that this segment of the Canadian population is undergoing at the present time.

5 The Pan-Indian Movement

The Native People's disillusionment with the religion and the legal, social, and educational systems of white society and the difficulties they have encountered when they have attempted to enter that society have led many of the younger generation to turn back to their native traditions. This returning to the old culture is gradually developing into a much wider movement. "Pan-Indianism" is being encouraged by a multitude of native organizations newly established in many areas of Canada and the United States. The individuals who form these groups are interested in maintaining all elements of native culture. An inherent difficulty in establishing this organization is the problem of forming a representative base for all Native Peoples across Canada, however. The Native Peoples have always found it difficult to support regional and national leaders who would act as spokesmen for all Native Peoples. The Lavall case well illustrates the points of view that separate those of native descent. Even within provincial organizations there is much bickering about what policies should be instituted. As Cardinal points out: "The Indian leaders found themselves coming to meetings year after year to be faced with the same resolutions. . . . They were unable to follow through on their resolutions."[1]

One of the factors that differentiate the Native Peoples from other ethnic groups, in the sociological sense at least, has been

1. Cardinal, op. cit., pp. 113-114.

their inability to evolve acknowledged organizations to serve as a power base. The Pan-Indian movement appears in some respects to be filling that role because the Native brotherhoods and national groups throughout Canada seem to be working toward a consensus, at least on some issues. The National Indian Brotherhood, which came into being in 1969, heralded the beginning of native unity in Canada. Although there is still much diversity within the organization, this can be seen as a healthy sign. To the present time, the National Brotherhood has been at the forefront of the movement seeking improved conditions for those of native descent. The difficulties they have encountered arise from a number of causes, including the difference between status Indians and non-status Indians (such as the Métis); the distrust that many Native Peoples feel towards the movement for national identity; and their fear that contact with those of Métis descent may jeopardize "their relationship with the federal government, and more importantly, endanger their treaty aboriginal rights."[2] The organization must also overcome a generation gap, as the older and more conservative of the Native Peoples tend to be sceptical about any movements that are considered radical or Red Power oriented.

Native groups in Canada have experienced difficulties similar to those encountered by the Blacks in the United States before the Supreme Court in 1954 decided that separate but equal education was an impossibility. This decision was of great importance for the Blacks because, aside from its immediate implications, it demonstrated to the Black community that the changes they saw as desirable were also attainable. Black organizations increasingly became Black in name as well as in membership for they learned to take pride in their racial heritage and no longer relied on, or in some cases trusted, support from the white community. From the mid-sixties until the present time, large sections of the Black community have continued to accept the existing legal and social system. Other parts of the community, however, have rejected the system because they believe that they should be able to enjoy the rights now enjoyed by other Americans. It is from this situation that the Black Power movement developed.

2. Interview with Mrs. Lavall, Canadian Press release, February 10, 1973.

Indian political power in Canada appears to be at an early stage of development. As the native population represents less than 2 per cent of the entire Canadian population, they cannot make the same dramatic impact upon Canadian society as the Blacks have made in the United States where they represent over 20 per cent of the population. In Canada, there are ten major tribal groups – eleven if one includes the Eskimos – and because of their geographical and social isolation these groups tend to be separated even more from each other than they are from the mainstream of Canadian society. However, probably inspired by the success of the Black Power movement in the United States, the Red Power movement is gathering momentum in many parts of Canada. An analogy between the Red Power movement in Canada and the Black Power movement must be drawn with caution, because, as R.C. Day maintains, Indian leaders generally have been unwilling to borrow from white or Black cultures without making substantial innovations of their own.[3] For example, Indians have organized hunt-ins and fish-ins during the closed season – something which had never before been tried. As in the United States, Indian activism has taken the form of blocking, protesting, and picketing against the laws and regulations of the dominant society. According to Day:

Specific obstructive tactics used by the Indians have included: 1) Delaying or halting dam construction, logging operations, customs collection, beach or island use, and use of negative stereotypes in advertising; 2) seizing control of, occupying, or obstructing use of government offices, military installations, border customs facilities, off-reservation fishing sites and "government surplus" islands; 3) non-violent picketing, speeches, sit-ins, marches and boycotts to pressure policy makers and gain public support; and 4) strong public verbal attacks against government officials or policies, such as jeering a Secretary of the Interior's speech and calling for his resignation. All of these actions involve violation of laws, organizational practices, or informal norms.[4]

3. R.C. Day, "The Emergence of Indian Activism," *Native Americans Today*, H.M. Bahr, B.A. Chadwick, et al., eds., New York: Harper Row, 1971, p. 513.
4. *Ibid.*, pp. 513-515.

The Native Peoples are trying to attain the rights guaranteed them by treaties and to gain public support for treaty rights. For the most part their tactics have remained non-violent. Within the native communities there is a large conservative element which maintains that the changes desired will come through an evolutionary process. This conservative perspective is dominant in the reserves, but as more of the younger, better educated Indians leave the reserves for the cities, it is likely that more militant demonstrations will occur until the Native Peoples have obtained their rights. Their message is simple:

They demand a return to basic Indian philosophy, establishment of ancient methods of government by open council instead of elected officials, a revival of Indian religions and replacement of white laws with Indian customs; in short, a complete return to the ways of the old people. In an age dominated by tribalizing communications media, their message makes a great deal of sense.[5]

At present the Red Power movement has not made a dramatic impact on the Canadian scene. It is possible that the Wounded Knee incident may have the same catalytic effect for Indians in this country as the Supreme Court decision had for the Blacks in the United States. So far, the main effect of the Wounded Knee incident has been broad publicity for the Native Peoples and their emerging activism; it has become an international symbol of successful assertion and challenge to the institutions of white society. Wounded Knee and the occupation of Alcatraz were early Indian challenges that provoked a thorough discussion of the implications of Red Power. Whether Indians are able to use the incidents as a basis for achieving their goals of self-determination is at this time a good point. There is no doubt, however, that the incidents served to give Indians on both sides of the border a positive sense of self-respect and group pride. This positive self-image is a major step forward for the Native Peoples, because they have to combat the negative image that the mass media in North America usually projects. Whenever

5. Deloria, "Country Better Off When Indians Ran It," H.M. Bahr, B.A. Chadwick, et al., op. cit., p. 504.

the Native Peoples in the past won a battle, it was termed a "massacre," but when government troops were successful, the results were always a "victory." Many people who are familiar with native history believe that the Battle of Little Big Horn was a massive victory for the Indians since General Custer previously had slaughtered Indians who had already surrendered peacefully. Mass military operations against the Indian peoples in Western Canada did not take place in the same way as they did in the States, due in no small part to the tactics of the Mounted Police. However, Canada's record is far from praiseworthy, for not only were the Beothuk of Newfoundland completely destroyed, but also many thousands of Indians across Canada were subjected to great hardships and cruelty at the hands of the newcomers.

In history, in popular fiction, and in films, the Indians are usually portrayed as heathens and savages. Native organizations are now agitating for a change in this stereotyped image, and, as can be seen in the renewed popularity of Grey Owl's books and from some of the more recent films, they appear to be having some success. Nevertheless, it will take considerable time to change both the image and the damaging social and psychological effects this image has had on the Native Peoples themselves.

One inescapable conclusion is the fact that the Native Peoples do not have a strong enough political presence to influence the mass media. One may expect, however, with the emergence of Red Power and such positive concepts as "Red is Beautiful," that the potentially damaging influence of the media may be lessened—especially if legislators become more attuned to the interests and difficulties encountered by minority groups. It is to be noted that the potential for control over the media leaves the government open to charges of restricting the freedom of the press, which is a sensitive point in North America. However, many people want control exercised to protect the Indians and other minorities from the negative stereotypes which frequently appear in the media.

The Judaeo-Christian value system upon which Canadian society is based is not responsive to the conditions of hardship and deprivation experienced by the Canadian native population unless these are dramatically demonstrated.

The difficulties experienced by this population are well-known, but the movements to rectify the situation tend to be slow and undirected. Many Indians, particularly those in Red Power organizations and groups, maintain that Indians themselves may be forced to take radical measures in order to make the Canadian government more aware and responsive to their needs.

6 Patterns of Urbanization

Like all newcomers, Native Peoples must go through a period of adjustment when they first come to an urban environment. They are faced with the conflicting influences of their traditional rural background and the expectations and realities of city life. Many of the physical, social, and economic problems that all new urban dwellers meet are felt even more severely by recent native migrants, since the disruption of their lives is in many ways greater than that of most immigrants. The majority of other immigrants do not have to change their previous economic and social position as radically as do the Native Peoples since many new immigrants, at least at first, settle in their own ethnic community in the city. The Native Peoples are more in the position of the first groups of immigrants of any particular ethnic origin, who usually encounter considerable difficulty when they first arrive. As Hauser and Schnore state:

> Each of the newcomer groups was in turn greeted with hostility, suspicion, distrust, prejudice and discriminatory practices. With the passage of time each of the newcomer groups climbed the economic ladder to achieve access to the broader social and cultural life of the community and increased general acceptability.[1]

1. P. Hauser and L. Schnore, *The Study of Urbanization*, New York: Wiley, 1965, p. 22.

Hauser and Schnore describe the similarity in patterns of residential distribution and social and economic positions of most new ethnic groups. Initially, most newcomer groups settle in the older and poorer downtown districts of the city; the longer the period of settlement, the more the groups tend to disperse and the further they move from the centre of the city. In the same way, those groups that have recently arrived have lower educational, occupational, and income levels than those groups that have been settled for longer periods.

It can be expected that the same pattern will be seen developing among the Native Peoples as more leave their rural environments and move into the cities. Although, of course, their problems will be different to some extent because of their greater visibility and different cultural characteristics, the same pattern of increased social and residential mobility should emerge. In discussing the urbanization of Native Peoples, it is not implied that this is a value necessarily worth striving for.

Partly by choice and partly by necessity, the majority of Indians have until recently remained on or near the reserves. William Kelly explained that since the Second World War however, and particularly in the fifties and sixties, more Native Peoples have been leaving the reserves and trying to establish a place for themselves in the larger society. The fact that many Native Peoples were in the armed forces during the War helped to stimulate this movement. In addition, not only are more Indians receiving a better education, but also the population on the reserves is rapidly increasing without any improvements in economic conditions or any expansion of work opportunities on or near the reserves.[2] Migrants of native descent, like other new urbanites, generally seek better lives in terms of positions, housing, education, and perhaps short-term goals such as entertainment, all of which they cannot easily obtain on the reserves.

The number of unskilled jobs in urban areas has been severely cut in recent decades because of technological innovations. Many Indians and others in similar low socio-economic positions, especially those in the unskilled categories, are unem-

2. W.H. Kelly, "The Economic Basis of Indian Life," *The Annals*, 311, May, 1957, pp. 71-79.

ployed because the labour market has not been able to adjust quickly enough to these changes, nor have more employers adapted to changes in the market. In either case, the effect on the worker is the same: structural changes in the economy lessen the demand for his skills while creating demands for skills he doesn't have. The technological changes occurring in industry mean that, although the labour force in general has increased substantially, the number of opportunities for professional, skilled, and white-collar workers has increased while those for semi-skilled or unskilled workers has declined.[3]

As a large proportion of Canadian Indians have not even completed elementary school, many of them qualify only for the steadily diminishing number of semi-skilled or unskilled positions available. This lack of job opportunities has lessened the attraction of the city for the Indians. However, research has indicated that North American Indians experience less prejudice and racial discrimination in large metropolitan areas than in rural communities.[4] In larger communities, the majority of the populace have rarely been exposed to direct contact with Indians so that, in many instances, the native retains his traditional romantic image in the eyes of the host population. In these areas, he is employable if he has the required skills, whereas in smaller communities, especially those near Indian reserves, the prevailing image of the Indian tends to be extremely negative and the opportunities available to Indians are limited. It is not uncommon to find that those of Indian descent who opt for urban living want to live in larger metropolitan areas because they feel they are treated more fairly there.

During the research done for the book *Indians in the City*, I visited most communities in Canada with a population of over 150,000. Like other researchers, I did not find that Indian neighbourhoods or "little reserves" had developed in these cities. As mentioned in the Introduction, Indians cannot be classified in the same ethnological and anthropological sense as can other North American minorities. Native Peoples do not form a distinct racial group since their geographical isolation has meant

3. Ontario Legislative Assembly, "Report of the Select Committee on Manpower Training," Toronto: Queen's Printer, 1963, p. 9.
4. Nagler, *Indians in the City*, *op. cit.*, p. 50.

that several differing patterns of culture have evolved. Their identification as Indians by an outside group, however, has had important effects on their subsequent group development.

On their arrival in the city, the Native Peoples often find that their limited education and lack of training place them at the lower end of the socio-economic scale. This, combined with the fact that those who have lived on reserves are frequently at a disadvantage because their value system is very different from the value systems and expectations of urban dwellers, usually means that they are most likely to settle in slum or semi-slum areas. Surveys of cities in Canada and the United States indicate that there are no native neighbourhoods or ghettos in the sociological sense, in spite of the fact that relatively large numbers of the Native Peoples may be found in lower socioeconomic districts.[5] Rarely do the Indians develop the institutional frameworks usually found in Italian, Chinese, or other ethnic neighbourhoods. The key factor is probably that the Native Peoples are not members of any distinct cultural, racial, or ethnic group, and to have racial or ethnic neighbourhoods, there must be an acknowledged common heritage among the members of the community. Only in a few cases, such as the Navajo relocation project in Denver, is it possible to transpose a group of Native Peoples from a reservation into a specific urban neighbourhood.[6] In most instances, the Native Peoples arrive in cities from a variety of locations and do not possess the common bonds that will enable them to unite in an urban community. In addition, most reserves are close to urban centres and many of the Native Peoples visit their reserves on a daily, weekly, or monthly basis even after they have moved to the city. The needs that an urban community fills for immigrants who are too far from their homelands to return easily or frequently are filled for the Native Peoples by their reserves, which continue to act as their social and cultural centres. In examining urban adjustment patterns, it appears that, in larger cities, the Native Peoples form several distinct groupings related not only to their occupation or profession, but also to patterns of association in and with

5. T. Graves, "Perceived Opportunities, Expectations and the Decision to Remain on Location," mimeograph, University of Colorado, 1965.
6. *Ibid.*

the urban centres. Some Native Peoples are permanent urban residents, while others live in the city for short periods of time. It is possible to differentiate the status patterns that develop among Indians who have chosen different types of urban association. The following four categories were developed from the results of research conducted primarily in Toronto, but with reference to other large Canadian cities, such as Vancouver, Calgary, Edmonton, Regina, Winnipeg, and Montreal, where the native population is rapidly increasing.[7]

 1. THE WHITE-COLLAR WORKERS

The white-collar group consists of a very small proportion of the urban native population, but it is spread over most professional positions. In many respects, members of this group have the same leisure patterns as non-native members of white-collar groups. Their attitudes toward their backgrounds account for the development of three distinct sub-groups: those who identify with their Indian heritage, those who are ambivalent about their native identity, and those who have rejected their Indian ancestry.

Those who readily identify with their heritage are becoming an active sub-group which is now intensely involved in promoting interest in native tradition. Their activities range from organizing Indian groups in the city to lobbying at municipal, provincial, and federal levels to improve the Indians' position. Many members of this sub-group are involved with the Pan-Indian movement in trying to bring together facets of native culture. Indian groups have grown remarkably since the beginning of the 1970's, and have helped to develop native pride through their cultural activities. These groups have fostered a number of young activist leaders of native descent. Until the 1970's, there were very few native leaders, and the few there were tended to be relatively passive in outlook. But recently, prompted by events in the United States and by the growing emphasis on ethnic pride among most North American minorities, some of the new leaders have become more radical.

7. Nagler, *Indians in the City, op. cit.*

Although the number of white-collar workers in the native community is small, their role in fostering the development of native institutions and activities has been of great importance. Many of the Native Peoples who have had an ambivalent attitude towards their ancestry are now being drawn into the more activist category, but there are still small sections of native urban populations who remain undecided about their status. Although they accept the label of "Indian," they tend to participate in non-native activities, believing that they will improve their position by associating with other urban dwellers.

Members of the third white-collar sub-group have been traditionally designated as the "passers." These people refuse to identify with any ancestral ties either because they believe that such connections will restrict their occupational opportunities and social mobility, or because their traditional ties are so remote that they identify more easily with whites than with Indians. The former see Indian identity as a hindrance to their acceptance in the urban environment; the latter simply cannot identify with their compatriots anymore. The phenomenon of "passing" is a common minority adaptation that has been illustrated in a number of studies on other minority groups, such as the Blacks, Italians, and Jews.[8] Minorities often opt to identify with the majority group because they believe that the stigma attached to them as a member of a particular minority will result in their being subjected to differential treatment.

2. THE BLUE-COLLAR WORKERS

In the research done for *Indians in the City*[9] it was found that there are very few passers among native blue-collar workers, although there are activists and those with an ambivalent attitude. The author of the study deduced that, because the blue-collar natives tend to have arrived more recently, they maintain closer ties with their former communities. In addition, being members of a lower status category than the white-collar work-

---

8. Drake and Cayton, *Black Metropolis*, New York: Harcourt, Brace and World, 1945; Gans, *The Urban Villagers*, New York: Free Press, 1962; and S. Rosenburg, *The Jews of Canada*, Toronto: McClelland and Stewart, 1970.
9. Nagler, *Indians in the City*, *op. cit.*, p. 84.

ers, they usually have had little previous contact with whites and therefore feel alienated from the white community. Another reason for the apparent lack of blue-collar passers is the fact that urban work patterns differ substantially from those on the reserve. In the city, work is separated from family and social life and the worker returns to his family at the end of the day. This may serve to reinforce the importance of primary reference group associations and deter the newcomer from making outside contacts apart from work.

Blue-collar native workers may be classified in two subgroups depending on their attitude toward their occupations: the committed, who regard their employment as permanent, and the uncommitted, who view their employment as temporary. Many of the native blue-collar workers who are not committed to their work have not adjusted to city life and have not accepted the work ethic of the average urban dweller. Members of this sub-group tend to live close to their home environment, or to visit friends from home frequently in the belief that their friends can help them get another job when necessary. In some instances, these uncommitted blue-collar workers maintain that they are being discriminated against as a result of their Indian ancestry, and that that is the main reason they quit their jobs so frequently.

The research for *Indians in the City* also showed that blue-collar Indian workers are inclined to believe that those who readily change employment are responsible for creating the negative stereotypes held about Indians. It appears that many uncommitted workers rationalize their own inadequacies by putting the blame for their constant unemployment on external sources.

However, an ever-increasing number of blue-collar workers are becoming involved in native pursuits in the cities. Like their white-collar counterparts, they are becoming intensely involved in native organizations that focus on cultural and community activities. There has been a rapid development in craft activities amongst the Native Peoples in urban centres during the last few years. In part, this may be explained not only by the increasing awareness of the importance of their identity, but by the financial support given by the federal government in the form of L.I.P. and Opportunities for Youth grants and, to a lesser extent, by provincial, civic, and private groups who are becoming increasingly aware of the plight of the Native Peoples.

3. THE TRANSITIONALS

The transitionals may be defined as those Native Peoples who are attempting to become permanent urban residents. Many of these are students who come to the city to receive training for advanced occupational and professional positions, and who want to establish permanent residence in the city. Once they have experienced the comforts of urban life, they see the reserve as less attractive, and many find that the skills they have acquired are not readily usable on the reserve.

Aside from students, some transitionals have come to the city to seek permanent employment, although many are unskilled and do not have the resources to enable them to live independently in an urban environment. Because the demand for unskilled labour has diminished rapidly over the last few decades, many have to return to the reserve. In some cases, however, "re-evaluation of what is required to survive in an urban setting may bring them back to the city."[10]

4. SHORT-TERM URBAN RESIDENTS

The preceding three categories of native urbanites may be differentiated from the following category in that the latter have no long-term commitment to urban living. These "urban users" are natives who come to the cities to fill short-term needs, such as to purchase supplies, to receive medical treatment, or for entertainment. Some do not stay in the city longer than is necessary, as they do not like the tempo of urban life. Others come to the city for medical treatment under the auspices of government agencies, and often have to remain for a long time. During these periods of rehabilitation some are able to become acquainted with the ways of the city even though they may never have desired to live in a larger community. Some of these people

10. *Ibid.*, p. 86.

attempt to establish permanent residence in the city, but they usually return to their reserves eventually. Their arrival in the city because of ill health rarely gives them the chance to establish or maintain relationships with people who could make adaptation to urban living easier for them.

Another sub-group of urban users are those who come to the city for the short-term purpose of "letting off steam." Being used to their system of mutual aid, they in many cases expect their urban friends to look after them, but their urban tribesmen cannot usually afford to do so. People in this sub-group are the ones who usually encounter difficulties with the law for drunkenness, vagrancy, and prostitution.

A further sub-group is that of the workers who come to the city during the spring, summer and fall months when economic activity is at its highest. Where possible, these seasonal workers continue to live on the reserves, since living expenses in many cities would be too high. In centres such as Vancouver, Calgary, Hamilton, and Montreal, seasonal workers are able to commute to their reserves on a daily basis, but in other cases they can commute only on a weekly or monthly basis. When staying in the cities they tend to live in the lower socio-economic areas; they rarely participate in city activities, as their web of affiliations remains based on the reserve.

The final group of short-term urban residents are the vagabonds who spend the spring, summer, and fall in rural areas doing agricultural work or following the stampede trail. In winter, they return to the cities and find temporary jobs to support themselves during the cold months.

Those interviewed in this category appear to be very adept at establishing relationships with non-Indians, and they are professionals in the art of living for free. They know where to acquire free meals, drink and accommodation.[11]

It is apparent that the reserve or rural areas tend to act as social or cultural centres for a large proportion of the Native Peoples who live in urban communities. The Native Peoples in the blue-collar and transitional categories, at least according to

11. *Ibid.*, p. 87.

Graves and Nagler, illustrate the effect of maintaining strong ties with the home environment. A few of those in the white-collar category also tend to sustain a partial relationship with their reserve in that they have opted for a "passing" identification with their native ancestry. Thus, in some situations in urban society, they deny their native backgrounds and keep quiet about their native friends.

Due to the rapid increase in the size of most metropolitan areas, it appears that some Indians, especially those living on reserves near metropolitan areas (such as Vancouver or Montreal), become urbanites simply by remaining on their reserves, since these areas are now being incorporated into the municipality. Dowlings, in his article, "A Rural Indian Community in an Urban Setting,"[12] describes a similar situation in Green Bay, Wisconsin. In this city, just as in Vancouver and Montreal, Indian communities have remained separate only because social distance has replaced territorial distance.

Where Indians opt for urban association, it appears that growing numbers of them prefer to move to the relatively large centres where they can become invisible if they wish to pass. In larger metropolitan centres they encounter much less opposition than in small communities where their ancestral identity prevents them from participating on an equal basis with the other residents.

Legislation in Canada concerning treaty and non-treaty Indians often seems to have deterred the growth of Indian institutions in urban areas. This is because many Indians who have chosen to live in the cities have taken advantage of the money to which they are entitled if they relinquish their official native status. The Canadian government has not yet developed schemes such as the Navajo relocation project in Denver, Colorado, where the American government helped to relocate a large group of Navajo in an urban area.

Rapid urbanization of Canadian Indians, however, appears to be an increasing phenomenon at the present time, with the result that Indian organizations are evolving in the cities. The Red Power movement and Pan-Indianism – potentially powerful

12. J.H. Dowlings, "A Rural Indian Community in an Urban Setting," in *Native Americans Today, op. cit.*, p. 478.

lobbies that will undoubtedly influence the direction of Indian policies in the future—are being fostered. However, the proximity of the reserve is still a great asset to many Native Peoples, as Bahr pointed out:

> In cities bordering on reservations the ready accessibility of Indian companions and the proximity of the reservation may operate to dilute the impact of the urban environment. It is hard for the urbanite Indian to "drown in the mainstream" when the reservation is only a half-hour away.[13]

Bahr and others have indicated that when an Indian attempts to move to a large urban centre he experiences a cultural and social shock similar to that felt by most foreign immigrants to North America. This shock is felt as a direct threat to his identity.

> A normal response to feeling of being "lost" in an alien culture is to seek out others like oneself and to reaffirm a threatened identity by celebrating common elements of the threatened culture. Thus the relocation of relatively unassimilated Indians to major urban centres far removed from reservations has tended to increase their sense of Indian identity, as well as teaching them the ways of the city.[14]

In Canada many native elders try to keep young Indians on the reserve to protect them from the "evils" of the city. In the last few decades, however, the Indians opting for urban life tend to be younger and better educated than those remaining on the reserves. They are better able to cope with the situation and to organize themselves. Bahr found that although Native Peoples were formerly divided, they are now beginning to overlook tribal differences "in the face of their common antagonist, the white man."[15] Their organizations are now beginning to make their influence felt, so that policy concerning the Native Peoples may become more native-oriented and native-directed.

13. H.M. Bahr, "An End to Invisibility," in *Native Americans Today*, op. cit., p. 409.
14. *Ibid.*, p. 410.
15. *Ibid.*

For many years, native urban migration tended to separate the migrants from their ancestral ties, but recently it has created conditions that have enhanced Indian identity. Growth of native life in urban areas can be seen in the development of Indian cultural and social organizations, and the increase of newspapers and books. In some areas, the Native Peoples have their own radio programs conducted in their native languages.

Thus the trend to urbanization, rather than continuing to destroy native identity, perhaps is beginning to have the opposite effect. Interest in native culture, with the help of Pan-Indianism, is starting to create a racial pride, which should help to erase the negative image of the Native Peoples accepted by so many during the last century. The Indian is no longer substantiating the belief that he is a fast-disappearing element of North American society, but rather, in part as a consequence of his urban experience, he is becoming an ever more important element not only in urban areas, but also in the national context.

As was said earlier, urbanization in itself is not a goal toward which all Indians should strive, for, as the Hawthorn Report demonstrates, there are some Native Peoples in rural areas who still can retain their traditional way of life. However, many of the difficulties that most Native Peoples have experienced in adapting to the twentieth century stem from the fact that they can no longer remain self-sufficient; they must turn to the larger society to earn a living. As Alan Borovoy discovered:

The poverty of the Indian staggers the imagination of the white man. It simply drains our mental resources to conceive of how in the technological Canada of 1966 over 80% of Indian homes are devoid of such elementary facilities as sewers, septic tanks, flush toilets, running water, and telephones.[16]

This poverty shows that Indians cannot be self-sufficient on their reserves, and it also limits their opportunities for successful adjustment to urban society.

16. A.A. Borovoy, "Indian Poverty in Canada," in *Poverty in Canada, op. cit.*, p. 213.

7 Patterns of Deviance

The extent to which any minority has adjusted to the larger society can best be gauged by how well it has assimilated and conformed to the folkways, mores, norms, and laws of that society. Those who have difficulty in adjusting often resort to various types of deviant behaviour in their attempts to establish a place for themselves in the alien society. These forms of behaviour often result in infractions of the law and convictions for drunkenness, vagrancy, prostitution, or petty theft. Criminal statistics in Canada show that the Native Peoples are overrepresented for such offences. In many areas the ratio of arrests is ten Indians to one white person. As Charles Reasons states, "the most prevalent explanation given for the high rate of American Indian crime is essentially economic determinism."[1] This comment can be applied to Canadian Indians as well as to those in the United States. At both provincial and federal levels the proportion of Indians to whites in penal institutions is far greater than their proportional representation in the population in general; and the standard of living for the majority of Indians is well below the average for Canada.

Many Native Peoples have been arrested for alcohol-related offences, but Reasons found that there is an increasing number of Native Peoples convicted of more serious crimes, such as auto

1. C. Reason, "Crime of the American Indian," in *Native Americans Today*, *op. cit.*, p. 323.

theft, robbery with or without violence, and larceny. Reasons maintains that

> ... except for specific non-alcoholic related offences, homicide, suicide, assault, burglary, larceny, auto theft and robbery, Blacks have the highest rate, followed by Indians with rates for both groups considerably above those of whites.[2]

In attempting to explain the high rate of deviant and criminal behaviour among the Native Peoples, one must take a variety of factors into consideration, including poverty, boredom, prejudice and discrimination, anomie, and the negative effects of the social welfare system. According to Reasons, the main causes, apart from economic factors, of the increasing crime rate among Native Peoples are anomie and cultural conflict—two related factors. Anomie is often a result of cultural conflict because, in a situation where the unclear and conflicting norms of an individual are not integrated with those of society in general, he feels no moral commitment to that society and therefore becomes deviant or antisocial in his behaviour. When legitimate access to his goals are blocked,[3] an Indian will often resort to illegitimate means to attain his ends. As Reasons explains:

> Behavioral disorders such as alcoholism and chronic hitting-out are most common among men who aspire to white-dominated positions and status without adequate means to fulfill these aspirations.[4]

It is frequently the case with the Native Peoples that, especially when they first come to the city, they see the better standard of living that the majority of the white population enjoys and feel that they also are entitled to this standard. However, the

2. *Ibid.*, p. 319.
3. R. K. Merton, "Social Structure and Anomie," *Social Theory and Social Structure*, New York: The Free Press, 1965, pp. 121-159.
4. L. Dizmang, "Suicide among the Cheyenne Indians," in *Native Americans Today, op. cit.*, p. 374.

majority of Native Peoples do not have the education or skills to get high salary work (See Chapter 6). Discouraged by their inability to get or keep good jobs with good wages, a high proportion turn to petty crime. This situation is not limited to the Native Peoples; if one examines most societies, one finds that those persons at the bottom of the socio-economic ladder are more likely to have records of conviction for petty criminal offences (such as drunkenness, vagrancy, or theft – which have come to be thought of as lower-class crimes.) In areas where the poor are further separated from the rest of the population by racial distinction, the incidence of crime and social disorganization tends to increase dramatically.

There are, however, factors other than perceived and relative deprivation that account for the high rate of deviant behaviour among the poorer element of the native population. One must also consider the effect of anomie and cultural conflict. As Donald Cressey points out, the Criminal Code usually reflects the moral standards of the dominant society:

> *Because all members of the society are not equally committed to the norms of the powerful, there is conflict which manifests itself in crime. An interpenetration of conflicting norms can occur in three ways: (1) codes clash on the border of contiguous cultural areas; (2) colonization brings imposition of one group's criminal law upon another; (3) one cultural group migrates to another area.*[5]

It would appear, as Arthur Riffenburgh maintains, that all three of these factors have combined to produce the conflict between Indians and whites in our society.[6] The laws and norms of white society have been imposed on the Native Peoples; but also on the part of both groups there is a lack of understanding of the laws and customs of the other, so that neither really knows what it is in the code of the other that is being transgressed. Thus Native Peoples may act in a way that is acceptable in their

5. D.R. Cressey, "Culture Conflict, Differential Association and Normative Conflict," in *Native Americans Today, op. cit.*, p. 324.
6. A.S. Riffenburgh, "Cultural Influences and Crime among Indians and Americans of the South West," in *Native Americans Today, op. cit.*, p. 324.

society without realizing that what they've done is an offence in the eyes of the whites; and, in turn, the whites do not realize that, to the Indian, his act is perfectly acceptable.

Of all the literature available on deviant patterns of Indian behaviour, perhaps the most extensive is on the use of alcohol, and alcohol-related offences. It must be stated that excessive use of alcohol among both whites and Indians is often the result of similar conditions, and has the same negative consequences for both groups. In attempting to understand the excessive drinking that takes place among many Canadian Indians, one must first consider some aspects of their culture. In the first place, excessive drinking among all North American Indians reflects a basic difference in social values compared to whites. According to Littman in his article, "Some Observations on Drinking among American Indians,"

> Drunkenness does not damage the Indian's self-image . . . alcoholism is not seen as a personal problem and there is no shame, guilt, or remorse following a binge.[7]

Alcohol was introduced to the Indians by the fur traders. As its use spread rapidly among the Indians it came to have more serious social, economic, and political implications – both for them and for the white men – than had ever been envisioned.[8] In explaining alcoholism among Indians, Dailey makes an interesting evaluation in terms of the quantity of alcohol that Indians apparently consume:

> Consider first their mode of eating, and especially their custom of consuming everything in one sitting. It becomes clear then that it was only the alcohol which was new, not the practice of consuming everything at once. Hence the brandy feasts as they were called were on the same pattern as the eat-all feast.[9]

7. G. Littman, "Some Observations on Drinking among American Indians," paper read at the 27th Congress of Alcoholism, Frankfurt, Germany, September, 1964.
8. R.C. Dailey, "Alcohol and the Indians of Ontario Past and Present," *Anthropologica 10*, Vol. 10, No. 1, 1968, p. 81.
9. *Ibid.*, p. 193.

It is the custom of Indians at their feasts to eat all of the food at one sitting. Anyone eating sparingly – even using poor health as an excuse – is rejected, and considered ill-bred and ignorant of the art of living.[10] Dailey suggests four reasons Indians drink. First, the physiological effects of alcohol provide a novel physical sensation. According to Dailey, many Indian people seem to feel that under the influence of alcohol they can become exceptional people, possessing unusual physical power and public-speaking abilities. Secondly, the Native Peoples feel that liquor helps them to have visions and dreams – experiences they value greatly. Through alcohol, the Indian can achieve a degree of ecstasy never before possible. Thirdly, there is the suggestion that some Indians use alcohol so that they will not be held responsible for acts of violence which they will otherwise suppress. Finally, as whites assume more and more control over Indian affairs, the former integrating effects of warfare and other village-wide activities are replaced by the search for and communal use of alcohol.[11]

To many Native Peoples, the consumption of alcohol has become one of the main sources of recreation. It also provides a strong motivating force for economic activity, for without money it is impossible to get liquor. For the Native Peoples, becoming inebriated is socially acceptable, and some drink for the sole purpose of getting drunk. There are few, if any, inhibitions against the use of alcohol, in contrast to white society, where guilt and stigma are often attached to inebriation. According to Dailey:

> ... the alcoholic problem for the Indian is not one that involves a threat to health — but rather an economic problem in that a greater proportion of cash income may be spent on drink rather than on the essentials of modern living.... The modern day Indian is not facing the problem of food shortage ... nowadays the Indian has a number of welfare agencies from which to derive the necessities of life if he

---

10. R. G. Thwaites, ed., *Jesuit Relations and Allied Documents*, Vol. 1, 1896, pp. 285-87.
11. Dailey, *op. cit.*, p. 200.

cannot afford to secure them for himself. Certainly, the Indian has a sense of security in so far as relief is readily available, but from the point of view of most whites, this is not a desirable situation.[12]

In many instances, native drinking is a social pastime which serves as a form of recreation and a response to the frustrations and boredom encountered not only on the reserve, but in urban centres as well. Studies by Dailey, Littman, and Brody indicate that those of Indian descent seldom drink alone, for much of the satisfaction is derived from the social environment where drinking takes place.

Ferguson advances some suggestions about Navajo drinking behaviour which appear to apply to the drinking patterns of many Native Peoples in this country. She maintains that some Navajo are recreational drinkers who consume alcohol just because it is one of the pleasures experienced in towns. These individuals are in danger of becoming alcoholic because of the strong pressures exerted by the drinker's peer group and because of a lack of sanctions in Navajo society against drinking. Lack of sanctions against drinking appears to be widespread in native communities in America, for as Ferguson points out, these drinkers tend to be "less directly involved in contemporary industrial society, although they may work away from the reservation for several months of the year in menial jobs."[13]

The second group of excessive drinkers that Ferguson cites are "anxiety drinkers who drink in response to stress." Frequently the better-educated and well-employed suffer most from psychological conflict as a result of contacts with the dominant society. As Slater and Albrecht recognized:

... extensive drinking among Canadian Indians has long been recognized as a major social problem. Non-Indian interest in the problem has been evident from the earliest attempts to outlaw the sale of liquor to Indians to the more recent concern over statistics showing that the proportion of

12. *Ibid.*, p. 31.
13. F.N. Ferguson, "Navajo Drinking: Some Tentative Hypotheses," *Native Americans Today, op. cit.*, pp. 345-57.

Indians arrested for alcohol-related crimes is higher than for any other group in the nation.[14]

Indians are concerned with the problem: various Indian tribal councils have voted for prohibitions on liquor even after the repeal of federal laws prohibiting the sale of liquor to Indians. Also there has been a "growth of nativistic and messianic movements strongly emphasizing the evils of drink, such as A.A. and the Native American Church."[15]

In spite of the fact that many Indians drink excessively, the results obtained in the research done for *Indians in the City*, as well as Dailey's and Littman's studies, indicate that, compared to whites, very few of the Native Peoples are admitted to hospitals or clinics with organic complications resulting from alcoholism. If anything, an Indian who drinks excessively is likely to develop tuberculosis and other diseases that strike when overindulgence and dietary deficiencies have lowered a person's resistance.

The Indians' manner of drinking and the social disapproval it provokes are changing gradually. In Canada at the present time, Indians may consume liquor legally, resulting in the gradual disappearance of the Indians' alley drinking and their habit of drinking all they can get at one time. Studies such as Nagler's and Dailey's have shown that although the legislation prohibiting the sale of alcohol to Indians has been repealed, there are still many Indians who may not be fully aware of this, for they remain secretive about their drinking and show considerable apprehension when questioned on such behaviour.

As Dailey points out, bootlegging has declined as the result of the changes in the law, but he noted that it is still prevalent on weekends and after hours. As he says:

> *. . . the major difference between Indian and white drinking patterns seems to lie not so much on what is consumed, but*

14. Slater and Albrecht, "The Extent and Costs of Excessive Drinking Among the Untah-Duray Indians," *Native Americans Today, op. cit.*, p. 358.
15. E.P. Dozier, "Problem Drinking among American Indians," *Quarterly Journal of Studies on Alcohol*, 27, March, 1966, pp. 72-87.

rather on attitudes towards its use. Many Indians drink to get drunk, although the reasons may be different. Nonetheless, drinking and drinking to get intoxicated remain a desired end. Little, if any, prestige falls on an Indian who can hold his liquor, nor do Indians compete with one another on drinking bouts to determine capacity.[16]

Another offence with which the Native Peoples are frequently charged is vagrancy, which is sometimes related to their excessive use of alcohol. Vagrancy has also been used as a "convenience charge" by some authorities to "rid the streets of undesirables." In many of the small communities in the country, some officials regard Canadian Indians merely as vagrants and public nuisances. In many instances, those charged do not understand that they have committed a crime, as they do not see why they must carry identification and show evidence of financial resources. A typical response is, "Who carries a wallet at home? There you don't need money anyway. I don't see why they needed to get me for that."[17]

Petty theft, creating disturbances, larceny, and prostitution are other common charges that Native Peoples frequently encounter. There also appear to be many incidents of homicide on reserves, but the local authorities have difficulty in solving these cases since many reserve residents are reluctant to co-operate with the police. In Vancouver, some Indians on Skid Row—especially the prostitutes—are involved with narcotics, but few Native Peoples in other large metropolitan areas are, probably because of economic and differential association factors.

Although the rate of suicide, apparently as a result of social disorganization, is rapidly increasing among the Native Peoples, suicide was practised among many North American tribes long before white settlement. In northern areas, it was traditional for some of the older people to be left alone after they could no longer maintain themselves in the expected fashion. In other areas, natives took their own lives because of broken love

16. Dailey, *op. cit.*, p. 195.
17. Conversation with a native in Toronto who had been convicted of vagrancy, October, 1971.

affairs or if they were unable to live up to expectations. Some died as a result of self-inflicted wounds during ceremonial observances such as the Sun Dance. It is, however, difficult to generalize on the rate and causes of suicide among Indians because of the diversity of their situations, as well as the differing cultural traditions evident in the eleven major groups of Canadian Native Peoples. Data now indicates that whereas previously suicide was most common among the older members of native societies, it is now becoming more widespread among the younger generation.[18]

Dizmang found that "acute alcoholic intoxication, family instability, social and emotional deprivation, multiple arrest records, youthfulness, low self-esteem, cultural conflicts, social disorganization, accident-prone tendencies, and overwhelming personal tragedies" all contributed to the higher suicide rate.[19] These factors combined in various ways to cause a pattern of social death which led to physical death. Dizmang's observations indicate that native suicide rates are a result of numerous misfortunes such as extreme poverty, family strife, rejection, and physical and mental cruelty which, in turn, are related to their minority status in this society.

As Bynum shows, Canadian as well as American Indians represent the classical sociological image of the marginal man:

> In brief, the marginal man is a person who participates in two different cultures without being totally committed to, or accepted by, either. Tension and maladjustment is often the result of bicultural loyalties. Originally, the concept was applied to the acculturation problems of Jews or other ethnic groups newly emancipated from the ghetto: and persons of mixed racial backgrounds. However, the concept and theory of the "marginal man" offers a framework for the understanding of Indian suicide. The American Indian, especially the younger generations, have become "marginal men." This condition has been caused by inadequate acculturation and assimilation of Indians into the ways and society of the white

18. Dizmang, *op. cit.*
19. *Ibid.*, p. 375.

man. *His marginality, in turn, has led to isolation, alienation, anomie, aggression, social disorganization of the minority subculture, and suicidal behavior.*[20]

The suicide patterns of Native Peoples, like other aspects of their deviant behaviour, may be interpreted in the Durkheimian tradition as being in the "anomic category." Anomic suicide occurs when the traditional normative structures that govern existence have been interrupted, and the population concerned is unable to integrate the alternative normative standards prevailing in society. It appears that the main reasons why certain minorities conform to or deviate from the established folkways, norms, mores, and laws of a society is determined by their levels of integration or non-integration. If one examines the Japanese, Chinese, or Jewish minorities in our society, one finds that they exhibit very low rates of deviant or criminal behaviour. This can be explained, at least in part, by the strong ties that unite these minorities in distinct sociological groups. The Native Peoples, as discussed earlier, have failed to attain this degree of internal cohesion. One would therefore expect that, as the Native Peoples become more integrated and assimilated in Canadian society, their rate of criminal or deviant behaviour will decrease. In addition, as they become more integrated, the labelling process will take a less heavy toll. However, at present many people of native descent are still labelled "Indian", with all the negative connotations that the label itself imposes. Negative images tend to be more acute in rural areas where conditions are more conducive to the exploitation of the Native Peoples. In fact, in these areas and, to a certain extent, in more urban areas as well, they experience difficulties with the law for activities which would not, for the most part, be considered offences had the offenders been members of the majority group. As Henshel and Henshel maintain:

By imposing the majesty of the law to label some few persons as deviant, the Indians are forced to surrender old roles and

20. J. Bynum, "Suicide and the American Indian," in *Native Americans Today, op. cit.*, p. 375.

self images, and to undergo unique experiences which, paradoxically from the standpoint of the intent of the labeller, may serve to heighten their deviant tendencies. Labelling thus focuses on the secondary deviation which may be brought about by society's reaction to the initial act.[21]

Canadian society, although theoretically valuing equality, has seldom if ever granted her minorities the advantages of "full Canadian citizenship status." Especially those that are more visible remain minorities in the sense that they encounter the barriers that minority status imposes.

21. R. L. Henshel and A.M. Henshel, *Perspectives on Social Problems*, Don Mills: Longman Canada Limited, 1973, p. 46.

Conclusion

Although sociologists have studied the effects of contemporary society on many of the minority groups in North America, they have not, as yet, conducted any extensive or systematic sociological investigations of the Native Peoples. The study of North American Indians traditionally has been the field of anthropologists. Perhaps in the past there has been grounds for this—until recently, most Indians have remained in closed societies that were ideal for anthropological research. However, as more and more Indians leave the reserves and attempt to enter the larger society, their situation falls more into the area of sociological rather than purely anthropological study.

As the Native Peoples come into contact with the larger Canadian society, they find it difficult to cope with sudden exposure to techniques of mass communications, and modern educational, economic, and political systems. In many ways, the difficulties they face are similar to those that the first members of any particular ethnic group encountered when they immigrated; and the way they are adapting to Canadian society is again similar to the process by which many of these minority groups became involved in the Canadian social structure. But whereas most immigrant groups could in part rely on their ethnic heritage to help them make the transition to the new society, the Native Peoples cannot. They are faced with additional difficulties because of their greater visibility; and unlike many other minorities, the Native Peoples do not share a common ethnicity, since they are defined as an ethnic group only by government agencies, through the *Indian Act*, and in the general public image of them.

Since they do not have a common ethnic heritage, they have experienced difficulties in evolving common goals, organizations, and leaders. Also, as the Native Peoples constitute less than 2 per cent of the total population of Canada, they have not made an impact on Canadian society through sheer numerical force. Many of the other ethnic minorities, such as the Japanese, Chinese, Ukrainians, or Jews, have come into conflict with the dominant group, but, because of their superior organization, they have been better able to fight for their legitimate rights. The Native Peoples entered the battle at a much later date, with far fewer resources, with a weaker organizational structure, and often with internal dissent. This, coupled with the racial discrimination they encountered, has resulted in many of the Native Peoples being left at the lower end of the socio-economic scale. From their past experiences, many Indians believe that the barriers to occupational mobility, political participation, education, and even citizenship are a consequence of prejudice and discrimination. However, the recent growth of Pan-Indianism and the Red Power movement are providing the impetus for greater national unity among these diverse people.

In terms of North American contact, the Native Peoples, "when seen in historical perspective are imbedded in transitory phases in a seemingly inexorable process."[1] This does not, however, necessarily imply that they will be completely assimilated into Canadian society. It is to be hoped that patterns of consensus on both sides will develop as new channels of communication are opened. Although many Native Peoples believe that they should be allowed to participate in and help to enrich the pluralistic structure of Canadian society, others feel that their adaptation to North American society inevitably means integration, amalgamation, and cultural genocide. These people view current integration pressures as a one-way process in which the attributes of their cultures are ignored. This denial of their

1. T. Shibutani and K.M. Kwan, *Ethnic Stratification*, New York: Macmillan, 1965, p. 571.

intrinsic value leads many to a sense of despair and the belief that they are still natives without a home.

Glossary

Anomie A state in which unclear, unintegrated, and conflicting norms define behaviour alternatives and the actor has no moral commitment governing the limits or ends of his action.

Collective Identity The perception of having a common heritage, including such factors as language, values, history, religion, common destiny.

Contagion A pattern of behaviour in which actors consciously or unconsciously imitate the behaviour of others because of model influence.

Deculturalization A condition whereby some groups lose elements of their native culture.

Ecological relationship The relationship of the group to its geographical environment.

Gemeinschaft A folk society characterized by primary relationships.

Isolative The process in which individuals or groups are isolated from the mainstream of a society.

Particularistic The process in which minorities are treated in a way different from other members of society because of their perceived differences.

Passing The process in which one's own identity is denied in an attempt to be accepted as part of another group for economic, social, psychological, or political reasons.

Universalistic A situation in which everyone, regardless of status, is accorded the same patterns of treatment.

Bibliography

Abt, L. and I. Stuart, *Interracial Marriages, Expectations and Realities*, New York: Grossman, 1972.

Bynum, J. "Suicide and the American Indian: An Analysis of Recent Trends," in *Native Americans Today: Sociological Perspectives*, edited by H. Bahr, B. Chadwick, and R. Day, New York: Harper Row, 1972.

Cardinal, H., *The Unjust Society*, Edmonton: Hurtig Press, 1970.

Cressey, D.R., "Culture Conflict, Differential Association and Normative Conflict," in *Native Americans Today, op. cit.*

Dailey, R.C., *Anthropologica* 10, No. 1, 1968.

Day, R.C., "The Emergence of Indian Activism," in *Native Americans Today, op. cit.*

Deloria, V., "Country Better Off When Indians Ran It," in *Native Americans Today, op. cit.*

Dizmang, L., "Suicides Among the Cheyenne Indians," in *Native Americans Today, op.cit.*

Dozier, E., G. Simpson, and M. Yinger, "The Integration of Americans of Indian Descent," in *Annals of the American Academy of Political and Social Science*, Vol. 3, May, 1957.

Elliot, J.L., *Minority Canadians: Native Peoples*, Scarborough: Prentice-Hall, 1972.

Ferguson, F.N., "Navajo Drinking: Some Tentative Hypotheses," in *Native Americans Today, op. cit.*

Hauser, P. and L. Schnore, *The Study of Urbanization*, New York: Wiley, 1965.

Havighurst, R., "Education among American Indians—Individual and Cultural Aspects," in *Annals of the Academy of Political and Social Sciences*, 311, May, 1957.

Hawelles, I., "Indians in Transculturation," in *Native Americans Today, op. cit.*

Hawthorn, H., *A Survey of Contemporary Indians of Canada*, Ottawa: Queen's Printer, 1957.

Henshel, R.L. and A.M. Henshel, *Perspectives on Social Problems*, Don Mills: Longman Canada Limited, 1973.

Keller, A.G. "Societal Evolution," in *Native Americans Today, op.cit.*

Kelly, W.H., "The Economic Basis of Indian Life," *Annals of the American Academy of Political and Social Science*, CCCXI, May, 1957.

Littman, G., "Some Observations on Drinking among American Indians," Paper read at the 27th International Congress of Alcoholism, Frankfurt, Germany, Sept. 1964.

McEwan, E.R., Indian Eskimo Association of Canada, Report of the Executive Director, June, 1972.

Nagler, M., *Indians in the City*, Ottawa: St. Paul University Press, 1970.

Nagler, M., *Perspectives on the North American Indians*, Ottawa: Carleton Press, 1972.

Patterson, E.P. II, *The Canadian Indian: A History Since 1500*, Toronto: Collier-Macmillan, 1972.

Reasons, C., "Crime of the American Indian," in *Native Americans Today, op. cit.*

Renaud, A., O.M.I., "Education from Within," unpublished manuscript.

Report of the Select Committee on Manpower Training, Ontario Legislative Assembly, 1963.

Riffenburgh, A.S., "Cultural Influences and Crime Among Indians and Americans of the South West," in *Native Americans Today, op. cit.*

Rogers, E.S., "Indian Time," Ontario Fish and Wildlife Review 4, 1965.

Shibutani, T. and Kwan, K.M., *Ethnic Stratification: A Comparative Approach*, London: Macmillan, 1972.

Simpson, G. and M. Yinger, *Racial and Cultural Minorities*, New York: Harper Row, 1970.

The Indian Act, RSC 1952, as amended by 1952, 1953, 1956, 1961 Department of Citizenship and Immigration, Ottawa, 2 (19).

Thwaites, R.G., ed., *Jesuit Relations and Allied Documents*, Joint Hearings before the Subcommittees of Interior and Insular Affairs, Congress of the United States, Eighty-third Congress, Second Session on S2750 and H.R. 7139, Part 7 (Flathead Indians, Montana), February 25-27, 1954, Termination of Federal Supervision over Certain Tribes of Indians, Washington: United States Government Printing Office, 1954, p. 819.

Vogt, Z., "The Acculturation of American Indians," *Annals of the American Academy of Social Science*, Vol. 3, May, 1957.

Zentner, H., "Reservation, Social Structure and Anomie: A Case Study," in A.K. Davis, "A Northern Dilemma," Reference Papers, Vol. 1, Western Washington State College, 1967.

Zentner, H., "Parental Behaviour and Student Attitudes Towards High School Graduation Among Indian and Non-Indian Students in Oregon and Alberta," *Perspectives on the North American Indian, op. cit.*

INDEX